David Broome

with Brian Giles

Twenty-Five Years in Show Jumping

Foreword by Sir Harry Llewellyn

Stanley Paul
London Melbourne Sydney Auckland Johannesburg

Stanley Paul & Co. Ltd

An imprint of the Hutchinson Publishing Group

3 Fitzroy Square, London W1P 6JD

Hutchinson Group (Australia) Pty Ltd
30–32 Cremorne Street, Richmond South,
Victoria 3121
PO Box 151, Broadway, New South Wales 2007

Hutchinson Group (NZ) Ltd
32–34 View Road, PO Box 40–086, Glenfield,
Auckland 10

Hutchinson Group (SA) Pty Ltd
PO Box 337, Bergvlei 2012, South Africa

First published 1981
© David Broome Ltd 1981

Set in Monophoto Baskerville
by Willmer Brothers Ltd, Birkenhead

Printed in Great Britain by the Anchor Press Ltd,
and bound by Wm Brendon & Son Ltd,
both of Tiptree, Essex

British Library Cataloguing in Publication Data

Broome, David
    Twenty-five years in show jumping.
    1. Broome, David
    2. Show jumpers, (Persons) – England – Biography.
    I. Title   II. Giles, Brian
    798'.25'0924   SF 336

ISBN 0 09 144410 1

In any sport there is always one person who, because of his unique ability and complete dedication, stands out among his fellow beings. David Broome is one such man.

BRIAN GILES

Contents

Acknowledgements

Thanks are due to Eamonn McCabe for his specially taken photographs including those of my son James; also to Bob Langrish for providing the bulk of the photographs and to the following for allowing the use of copyright photographs: Central Press, Colorsport, Phil Harris, Keystone Press Agency, E. D. Lacey, Peter Roberts, Sport and General, Tyne Tees Television, Steve Yarnell.

The colour picture of David Broome on Mister Softee is by E. D. Lacey, all other colour photographs are by Bob Langrish.

Foreword

David Broome was born in the same year as Foxhunter – 1940 – and lives fifteen miles from my home. His father Fred and I used to compete against each other just after the war and I saw a lot of David when he was the '*enfant terrible*' of the junior classes, winning everything. I last rode for Britain in 1957, when Aherlow obliged with a final clear round for the team in Rome, and I consider myself lucky not to have had to compete against David.

Later, as chairman of the selectors, I had the greatest difficulty in persuading him to go to Rotterdam at the beginning of his international career. He said he was not good enough; Fred thought I was throwing him in at the deep end. After endless arguments, they finally relented and David won the first event with Wildfire and Ballan Silver Knight in a two-horse class.

As this story shows, David has inherited the Scottish caution of his charming mother and a deep-rooted sense of horsemastership from his father. He never overfaces his horses, has great affection for them and never jumps them when they are not well. This is why Sportsman, Philco and the others go on winning year after year.

No one is better able to maintain complete accuracy at a fair, cadenced pace than David Broome. He can see his horse's stride many lengths away – sometimes round the corner – and he is able to make the necessary, almost invisible, corrections so that the final approach is balanced. The death in the ring of Manhattan last year upset him more than most appreciated and he still grieves for this courageous horse to whom he was devoted.

Since the 1972 Olympiad the Federation Equestre Internationale has put its house in order by introducing a world-wide system of licensed professionals and amateurs with permits. Many other Olympic sports would be wise to follow suit while the Olympic Games still requires amateur status. Although now denied the chance of an Olympic gold medal to add to the individual bronze medals he won in Rome in 1960 and Mexico in 1968, David Broome has reached the top of the professional tree. This, of course, has involved him in some controversial issues and while I do not necessarily agree with some of his points of view, I respect what he says.

David is on the executive committee of the British Show Jumping Association and has proved wise and far-sighted in counsel, realizing, no doubt, the importance of maintaining a healthy amateur element in show jumping without which the professional side would founder. Few international competitors can travel the world as true amateurs and perhaps the equestrians are luckier than most, as it is the owners and sponsors who have to bear the chief expenses incurred in the purchase and maintenance of top-class international horses.

As a star of his own making, David willingly fulfils his responsibilities to young amateur riders. He is unfailingly helpful and his advice is freely given.

Brian Giles, who helped David with this work, is one of the top-flight sports journalists with a nose for news. Sometimes we say, 'How the hell did he get hold of that?' but one cannot disguise the fact that he is a free thinker and a free writer who ever widens his readership and the circle of those interested in show jumping.

I wish them both the best of luck with this book.

HARRY LLEWELLYN

Introduction to a Champion

When a man has been at the top of show jumping for twenty-five years, he commands respect not only from other riders but from the public as well. David Broome is a household name known and appreciated by people all over the world, many of whom know little or nothing about the sport. They understand, however, that he rides horses, is a master at what he does, and keeps on winning. Like good wine he goes on improving with age, which gives his multitude of fans a very valid reason to overindulge their enjoyment of his talents, and the connoisseur the regular opportunity to savour the delights of something rather special.

To record every one of his many successes since he began his career would take the brain of a computer, the staying power of Arkle and a book three times the size of the Holy Bible. We can, however, take a close look at the man, study his talent in depth and seek to find the answer to the question that most people ask themselves at one time or another: 'What makes him so good?'

Over the years, and in many different countries, I have tried to analyse the ingredient which most of us lack and yet he has in abundance. But I have reached the firm conclusion that I have been chasing a dream because he was born with the genius he has, and no force on earth can alter that fact. All we can do is sit back and enjoy the pleasure he gives when he mounts a horse and takes it into an arena.

And, unlike many, David has been doing just that since the early days when names like Wildfire, Ballan Silver Knight, Discutido and Bess would spring to mind whenever his name was mentioned. It must also be remembered that in his teens he had to take on and beat people like Raimondo and Piero d'Inzeo, Hans Winkler, winner of two individual world titles and a handful of Olympic gold medals, and the great American, Bill Steinkraus.

It was in 1961 that he showed the world that he was a force to be reckoned with when in Aachen, West Germany, he won the European Championships on Sunsalve and left Piero d'Inzeo and Winkler trailing in his wake. As far as major titles were concerned, David had

David Broome on Bess, Hickstead, September 1965

arrived in the big-time and was to go from strength to strength, as he proved six years later when winning the European title again on Mister Softee, this time in Rotterdam, and two years later on the same horse at Hickstead, in Sussex. No other man has won the title three times. The record still stands and is likely to do so for some considerable time to come.

Although he didn't know it then, a year later he was to reach the pinnacle of his dazzling career when riding Beethoven to victory in the 1970 Men's World Championships, held in La Baule, France. To succeed where everyone else from Britain had failed was, indeed, a great achievement, and to win he had to compete on four different horses in the final. They were Beethoven, owned by Douglas Bunn of Hickstead, Graziano Mancinelli's Fidux, Harvey Smith's Mattie Brown and Alwin Schockemohle's Donald Rex.

Never before had I seen a horse as strong as Fidux, from Italy, who then looked as though he could have pulled the arms out of Samson had he had a desire to do so. All riders had to compete on each other's horses and only had a minute or so to warm up on them. When David's turn came for Fidux, those of us who were watching remained totally silent and had fingers crossed, but our fears were groundless because he gave Fidux a beautiful ride and later went on to win the title.

Mancinelli finished second, Harvey Smith third and Alwin Schockemohle, now retired from riding, fourth. Ten years earlier, it must be recorded, David had finished third in the World Championships, won by Raimondo d'Inzeo. That time he partnered Sunsalve, while the Italian rode Gowran Girl.

It was on Sunsalve in 1960 that David won his first King George V Gold Cup, open only to male riders and one of the most sought-after prizes in show jumping. If a competitor wins it once, he is justifiably proud and his name goes into the record books. Any statistically minded fan with a brain for dates will see the name D. Broome listed no less than four times. He won on Sunsalve in 1960, Mister Softee in 1966,

Sportsman in 1972 and Philco in 1977. If he keeps on going like that, the organizers of the competition will have to rename it after him.

Apart from his personal achievements, he is a great team rider who has helped his country to many triumphs in Nations Cups. Since 1965 Britain has won the President's Trophy nine times – far more than any other nation – and David has more than played his part in those successes. When a clear round can mean the difference between victory and defeat, he is the man most likely to be asked to pull something extra special out of the bag. This is because one of his best qualities is being able to remain calm under extreme pressure and get the best out of his horses when it really matters.

Only a person who can think deeply about what he is doing at such a time and remain totally in control is any use to a man like Ronnie Massarella, who has led British teams to victory on numerous occasions both in England and abroad. As a chef d'équipe he is, perhaps, unique because once he says he will do something, he does do it, and usually does it again and again. He is the first to admit that David is more than a little special where show jumping and, in particular, his teams are concerned.

Like that other great Welshman, Colonel Sir Harry Llewellyn KBE, David was honoured by her Majesty the Queen when he was awarded the OBE for his services to sport. It was a fitting reward for a man who had put so much into show jumping, and a time of joy for all the members of his family who support him in everything he does and who are always on hand to offer help and advice when it's needed. They are, indeed, people united by one common denominator – the love of the horse.

That is one of the main reasons the jumpers he rides go on giving of their best week after week, month after month, and season after season. Without proper care and attention, the long, hard battles they fight in the international arena would cause many of them to wilt with fatigue and eventually sink into obscurity. That, however, does not happen. And those searching for the secret of his success would do well to take note of that fact, because, without kindness to, and complete understanding of, horses, a rider is just one of thousands who can sit in a saddle. To win and become a champion takes a special breed of person who has those elusive qualities which make him a thoroughbred, fit to stand his ground among the greats and well out of reach of those wallowing in the mire of mediocrity.

Because he is a professional, David cannot ride in the Olympics unless the International Olympic Committee turn several somersaults, alter the rules and make the Games open to both amateur and professional riders. The chances of that happening are extremely remote: I doubt that its members are supple enough for acrobatics and, anyway, they are not very enthusiastic about deviating from the original concept. But David has good cause to remember with feeling the Olympics he has ridden in, particularly those held in Rome at the Piazza di Siena in 1960, when he won a bronze medal on Sunsalve.

On that occasion, many of those who watched his round were horrified when David went clear and then, ten minutes later, officials announced that Sunsalve had incurred a penalty at the water jump. He still won the bronze but, without that late appeal, it might well have been a higher award. Four years later he went to Tokyo but was out of the placings on Jacopo, and then, in Mexico in 1968, he again won the individual bronze on Mister Softee. At the ill-fated Munich Olympics in 1972, when several Israeli athletes were shot down by members of the Black September terrorist group, David finished fourteenth on Manhattan when the horse didn't perform as well as it should have done.

Eight months after that, he discarded his amateur status, turned professional and leased four of his horses to Esso for one year. When that contract ended in 1975 he formed a lasting friendship with Phil Harris and started riding horses owned by his company – Harris Carpets – a dynamic organization whose chairman has

David Broome won the bronze medal at the 1960 Olympic Games in Rome behind Raimondo and Piero d'Inzeo

a deep love and understanding of show jumping.

David and Harris proved to be a formidable combination and in the October of that year they devastated their opponents at Wembley's Horse of the Year Show by taking seven of the

13

major competitions held there and being placed in several others. David's rare riding ability linked with the mathematical brain of Phil Harris is the perfect formula for a sport which requires split-second timing and an awareness of what is happening at any given time.

That was certainly true in the World Championships in West Germany, when both men made their way to Aachen to try to win the title. The horse they relied on was the brilliant Philco, who was bred in America and who had rapidly made a name for himself in Britain. After many battles, against the strongest of opposition, David finally finished sixth, but he helped the British team win its gold medal and he and the other riders – Caroline Bradley, Derek Ricketts and Malcolm Pyrah – came away happy. They were all in tremendous form and the following season the quartet teamed up again, led by David on Queensway's Big Q, to mount a challenge on the European Championships held in the beautiful Kralingseweg arena in Rotterdam. The show started on Thursday, 16 August, with two optional competitions which did not count towards the actual championships. These particular events were used as warm-up classes to allow both riders and horses the opportunity of testing the ground and obstacles, later to be faced in the championships.

There was never any doubt about the individual favourite for the title: Gerd Wiltfang, of West Germany, who had won the World Championships in Aachen riding a horse of enormous quality and depth called Roman – an eight-year-old whose great strength was being able to jump brilliantly and produce top form again and again. Roman had already shown that the World Championships had not taken too much out of him by winning the Hamburg Jumping Derby prior to making his appearance in the European event.

The first leg of the championship was run over fourteen fences and, if a rider knocked one down, a penalty of 6 seconds was added to his final time. It was not, however, to be David's day because, when Queensway's Big Q entered the arena, he didn't appear to be concentrating on the job in hand and proceeded to clout fences two and thirteen.

The second phase of the championship was run over two rounds, again of fourteen fences, but this time built on the lines of those used for Nations Cup competitions, and time did not count, provided all riders went round in the time allowed for the course.

Derek Ricketts on Hydrophane Coldstream went clear followed, when her time came, by Caroline Bradley partnering Tigre. They, too, were faultless. But, once again, Queensway's Big Q seemed to be thinking of other things and, while David worked furiously to conjure up the best in him, the grey whacked the very first fence and hit part of the fifth obstacle. Malcolm Pyrah, who was the third member of the team to compete in this round, on Law Court, had also hit two. Everyone who had made the trip from Britain to Holland to watch was beginning to worry somewhat and wonder where the magic had gone.

The British, however, are renowned for their fighting qualities and never go down without putting up a battle royal. In the second and final section, Ricketts started and then stopped because the bell had sounded before the course had been finished. But that did not put off the rider and he and his mount eventually went round clear. All looked well with Miss Bradley, too, until she and Tigre hit two elements of the treble and recorded a total of 8 faults for the round. It was then left to Malcolm Pyrah and David to go clear and win the team title. The strain of being in such a position is enormous and only those with vast experience and an undying ambition to win fail to crack under this kind of pressure.

Pyrah, measuring every fence perfectly, steered Law Court to his clear and left the last and final detail to David. But although he didn't know it at that moment, the advice he gave to David was to prove invaluable.

15

Winners of the 1979 European Championships team event in Rotterdam. Left to right: David Broome on Queensway's Big Q, Derek Ricketts on Hydrophane Coldstream, Malcolm Pyrah on Law Court and Caroline Bradley on Tigre

Queensway's Big Q had been dragging its near-side foreleg on take-off at many of the fences and Pyrah had suggested that maybe a practice pole angled to the left might just cure the problem. When David came in to ride for team gold we all waited in anticipation, hoping that his horse would suddenly produce the form we knew he most certainly had but had yet to show in Rotterdam.

Although the horse rattled a couple of bars, David had him perfectly balanced and galloped through the finish with a zero score. The fantastic four were kings of the arena once again and perhaps the proudest man of all was Ronnie Massarella. All along he had said they would win, even when the situation looked less than good and once again his solid loyalty to those under his command had been more than justified.

He has seen many good riders, in countries all over the world, but what he says about David, Malcolm, Derek and Caroline must be recorded because, coming from such a respected member of the show jumping world, it has much more than ordinary meaning.

'They never give up, even when things look hopeless and that, really, is what it is all about. It is the best team Britain has ever had.'

For many years, David has played a major role in show jumping and has helped to make it what it is today – a major international spectator sport watched and enjoyed by millions.

This book is a tribute to him, his family, horses and all those who have helped him, in their own way, to reach and stay at the top.

1 The Horses I Ride

In all equestrian sports, including show jumping and eventing, a rider can make a big name for himself and become a national sporting hero if he has the horses who can keep on winning. Without them, his chances of success are remote and many who have set their sights at the highest level often find that they have to be satisfied with lesser ambitions. The old saying that 'it's tough at the top' is very relevant when applied to the world of show jumping.

When you reach the summit it is hard to stay in that rarified atmosphere and the only way to do it is to make sure you buy the right jumpers, and keep them 100 per cent sound when you have found them. David is no different from the rest in this respect and has travelled throughout Europe and America with his owners and advisers looking for the horses a man in his position requires. Since he is such a well-known personality, that is not always as easy as it may sound because, once the word is out that David Broome is interested in a horse, those who may be selling start talking telephone numbers and make the job that much harder. People who react like this, however, are dealing with experts who know the exact value of a horse and what it will be worth to them – experts like David's father Fred, and Frank Kernan from Crossmaglen, whose own son James won the 1974 Junior European Championship and has helped Ireland win many major competitions

James Kernan, 1974 Junior European Champion, whose father Frank is one of the experts David Broome calls upon when buying horses

since; they make a formidable team and are very rarely wrong.

David knows how important these people are to him, and he remembers in detail how and where each of the horses was bought and their characteristics, as he describes below. One of the most amazing characters he has ridden is the big grey gelding Queensway's Philco, who was bought in America.

Queensway's Philco

'Philco is very friendly and very kind but, you know, he is a rough devil with his head. In the stable he will knock you on your backside with it. I'm sure he's only being playful, but it does hurt at times. It is the only aspect about him that is different. When I'm standing in his stable, or the collecting ring, he'll bring his head round and wallop me and sometimes I don't even know what day it is. But he is a super horse.

'We got him from Rodney Jenkins in Florida in 1973 when Phil Harris, Frank Kernan and myself went out there with the sole purpose of buying horses. When we arrived I saw this big grey jumping and found out that Rodney, one of the top riders in America, had only bought him the day before. But we still watched him for ten days even though, at that time, we were looking for a good 'Open' horse to bring back home.

'Well, we looked and looked and in the end couldn't see anything we liked apart from the grey and it was Phil who eventually said, "Come on, let's buy him."

'He must have been the most expensive young horse ever to leave America but, after Phil had talked with Frank, there was no doubt in his mind at all. After that, what else could we do but call him Philco! We knew he had raced on the flat in America and some people told us that he had blue blood and was out of a horse by Raise A Native, who had won a lot of money. I couldn't care less and never did bother to find out exactly what he had done. It didn't matter

Philco at the Wales and West Show

at the time and it still doesn't because Philco has proved his worth over and over again. What I do know is that he was a very expensive yearling at the sales.

'The amazing thing is he was competing for several months but nobody bothered to buy him until the owners took him to Florida and Rodney Jenkins stepped in. Then we came along and when I saw him I couldn't believe my eyes. He was giving everything feet to spare and never ever looked like making a mistake. You just couldn't criticize him as far as that was concerned.

'Well, Phil bought him and we arranged to have him transported back to our stables and, after a while, I decided to take him to the Badminton show and try him out there. As far as I was aware, he had won £100 in America and I registered him with the BSJA as doing so.

'But that was a mistake to start with because, when I did finally check out his winnings, I found that all he had ever won in America was a total of $12. And here I was, jumping him in a £100 class when he was qualified to go in Foxhunters.'

It was at this Badminton show in Gloucestershire that Phil Harris and all those interested and concerned with the horse were to see exactly how good he was, because he proceeded to jump the opposition silly and ended the competition with two clear rounds and the beginnings of a big reputation. The word spread that David had found a new star, and anyone who was anyone at the time started to sit up and take notice of the new recruit from Florida.

'It was incredible,' said David. 'And, of course, Phil was delighted with what the horse had done. After all, he had made the final decision about buying him and he had a right to feel pleased with himself, as did Frank Kernan. Well, we have all come a long way since those times and when I was looking at his record of wins I discovered that he had won £100,000. That is a bit different from the $12 in America.

'He's thirteen now but a better horse you would have a job to find. He will jump everything, and is always willing to give his best. A perfect gentleman as far as I'm concerned, who eats everything you care to give him.'

Phil Harris had no doubts about the horse's ability right from the start and does, without any doubt, admire him greatly. 'From the very first I had a feeling that he was the one, even though it took us a few days to buy him. He most certainly is my favourite. And that is not just because he has won £100,000, but because he has always done everything we have asked him to do and never stops trying. An owner may find a horse who is good at any time – but Philco is not just good, he's great, and I don't think I will ever buy another one quite like him.'

Whenever business allows, Phil Harris and his wife Pauline travel from their home in Orpington, Kent, to visit the Broome family and the horses they sponsor. They are both deeply involved with show jumping, have a great admiration and respect for David and his family, and do more than enough for the sport they both love. It is this keen appreciation of what is going on all the time, that makes them so popular with all of those who either make a living in show jumping, or just take part for fun. 'When we find time the first thing we think about is show jumping and we go to as many meetings as we can. We like being owners and we most certainly like to see our horses competing. Of course, it is great when they win, but there is just as much pleasure watching David competing on them.'

Very few people would argue with that, but it is not often that David is not winning. It might not always be on Queensway's Philco because his back-up team of horses have to have their chances too.

Queensway's Big Q

Another horse Phil Harris purchased – in 1978 – was Queensway's Big Q who, when he was competing in West Germany, was given the delightful name of Golden Ass.

'That didn't fill us full of encouragement,' laughed David. 'And we did, of course, change it the moment we bought him. We got to hear about him from a dealer called Axel Wochener, who had been looking for a horse for us for some time. He told me that he had it on price for me and would I fly out to Dortmund and watch it competing in a show. I went there and saw it jump, but on the final day of the show the person who was selling him suddenly had a change of mind. You can imagine how I felt about that and I returned home very disappointed.'

In the world of horses, that sort of thing happens all too frequently and David had to wait another fourteen days for the move which was to set the wheels of business turning again.

'I had just walked into my parents' house after a long journey from Gothenburg when the phone rang. It was Axel, who was yelling down the phone that he had the horse on price again and would we return to Germany. Well . . . I thought about it, then decided to ring Phil and tell him what had happened. Whenever a horse is costing a lot of money, and he is spending it, I always like him with me. I think that is only fair. So off we went yet again, with my father accompanying us to watch the horse compete. Within half an hour of arriving, we had bought him.'

Although all are experts where horses are concerned, it was a fairly rapid decision to make because usually a horse is taken away on loan, tried out and, if he doesn't come up to expectations, sent back again immediately. David has never operated in this fashion and it does, at times, worry him.

'Actually, I think I must be crazy because whenever I buy a horse I usually just pop them over two fences. We tried Queensway's Big Q in the indoor school owned by the lady who was doing the selling: anyone who knows what he is doing will tell you this is totally wrong. I just jumped him over one parallel and a vertical; he was strong but I thought I could correct that with schooling at home. He was also a bit careful but I liked his jumping and at eight he was young enough.'

The deal was finally done and the trio

Queensway's Big Q during the 1979 European Championships in Rotterdam

returned to Britain without the horse. He was to follow on once the money had been transferred from England to Germany. That was to take a total of seventeen days and Queensway's Big Q arrived at David's stables just forty-eight hours before the Badminton show in Gloucestershire.

The Badminton estates are owned by the Duke of Beaufort, and the show jumping and three-day events there, which are run at the same time, are sponsored by Whitbread. On the Saturday of the show, the eventers ride across country while the show jumpers are performing in the main arena. It is a time when thousands of people flock to Badminton and this particular occasion was no different from other years. At least 150,000 fans turned up to watch the eventers and the grounds of Badminton House were thick with supporters.

This was Queensway's Big Q's first show in England, and it was a disaster. The horse knocked several fences down and was eventually pulled up.

'The whole community knew that we had bought an expensive horse, and when we had that disaster at Badminton I knew that I had been totally unprofessional. I should have had him going well at home before asking him to venture to a show. I always feel that many of those in the sport have a little gloat when things go wrong, but I didn't take it too much to heart because I knew the reason. And, anyway, everyone has good horses going badly at times.

'I am, however, a great believer in not buying horses on trial because, if we had on this occasion, we would most certainly have sent him back to West Germany. But our money was down and we had a problem. It was a case of going back to the drawing board.'

Those were agonizing times for both David and Phil Harris but neither lost faith in the horse they both knew had ability but was, for some unknown reason, loth to produce it. Queensway's Big Q is utterly genuine – of that there is no doubt – but the key to his brilliance has yet to be discovered. Many racehorse trainers are faced with the same problems, and will lose thousands of pounds buying horses from abroad only to find they cannot settle to their new surroundings immediately. Many take months, or even years, to reproduce the form they showed at home and there is nothing more frustrating or disconcerting for the trainers when they cannot discover what is wrong.

In most cases it is just a matter of being patient until everything comes right, but racing trainers and show jumping riders must have good owners who understand the problems and are prepared to wait, even though it may mean losing money by doing so. In this respect David is very lucky because Phil Harris is very much aware of the situation and backs his rider's judgement to the hilt. Phil knows that David has his interests at heart. It is a good relationship to have when the hard times come and is one of the reasons they have managed the long, frustrating climb to the top together.

'We still haven't got Queensway's Big Q right but, even though he is different from the others, we just keep on trying with him. There won't be a better horse once we get the programme right – of that I am sure. After all, he has won something like £40,000 and that's not bad for a horse who hasn't yet found his true form.'

Even though things haven't been exactly as they should be with Queensway's Big Q, David has plenty of memories of the fine performances the horse has put up, including a couple of very good successes abroad.

'He won two super Grands Prix with me in the winter of 1979, one in Brussels and the other in Bordeaux. Then he came back to England and competed in Olympia's Christmas international and finished third in the Grand Prix there. So he has got it in him. He's fast and can jump enormous fences and has all the scope in the world. But he can be an absolute goat – there is no other way to describe him: when he's good, he's brilliant; but when he's bad, he's horrid.'

Though David describes the horse in this manner, it doesn't mean that he dislikes him. He has a great respect for all the horses he rides, but at the same time he is pragmatic because he has to be. He knows that, once he finds the answer to the problem, the horse will show top form and that is why he, and everyone else connected with the animal, is being patient – even though it can, at times, be infuriating.

This is one of the aspects of show jumping that very few people who watch the sport understand. If David or any of the leading riders is beaten, they are thought to have lost their touch. But nothing could be further from the truth. The riders have just met with a few problems which, with luck and expertise, they will solve. It is always nice to keep on winning but even champions have to be unplaced on occasions.

Another equally important factor to remember is that the horses they ride are not machines and cannot be switched on and off like car engines. They have their own feelings and there are periods when they cannot, or will not, produce their best. And, if those who are looking after the horses cannot understand this, then they will quickly be heading for oblivion.

Queensway's Sportsman

Queensway's Sportsman is, and will always be, David's favourite and anyone who has ever seen them compete together can easily understand why. Instead of being just horse and rider, they move as one powerful, swift-flowing force, and it is this which David so much appreciates about him.

'He has a beautiful, natural balance and perfect rhythm. He's the sort of horse everyone dreams about.

'I bought him in 1970 from my old friend Frank Kernan, who rang me from Ireland one day and asked me if I would go over and have a look at some of the horses he had in his yard. I'll never forget it, actually, because it was one of the bitterly cold days which seem to go right through to the bone. After a good night's sleep at Frank's place, I got up, had some breakfast and waited for the horses to be shown to me.

'Frank's practice area was just outside the

Queensway's Sportsman at the Birmingham International Show Jumping Championships, April 1980

kitchen window and, as I watched one of the horses was being hacked about and coming in to jump a 2 foot 6 inch high pole. Well, if I told you the bells rang and the lights flashed when he jumped that pole, you will have some idea of what it meant to me. Everything was right about him. Even young Ned Cash, who was riding him at the time, came over to me afterwards and told me he didn't understand why they were selling him and added that he was one of the best horses he had ever sat on. And, when I got on him, I knew exactly what he meant. I had to have him.'

But for anyone looking for a horse the worst thing they can do is leap right in and point out the one they want. The dealer then knows how much it means to the prospective buyer and will get the best deal he possibly can. That is completely fair and common practice in business. The buyer must take time, haggle over the price, and appear as though he doesn't

really know if he wants to buy or not. It's all a question of getting the best value possible and David knew this from experience.

'It took me all day to do the business and my problem was trying to buy him without Frank really knowing that he was the one I wanted. So we talked and talked and finally the deal was done to everybody's satisfaction. To be fair to Frank, though, he showed me five very good horses and, when I think about it, I should really have bought a couple more while I was out there. . . .

'When I got the horse back home, I had to go off to a reception in London. Normally I never go to gambling clubs or anything like that, but this reception I attended was held at the Sportsman's Club. And, when I saw the name over the door, I knew the horse I had just bought was going to be called "Sportsman" – it just sounded right and seemed to suit him.

'In the April I took him to Hickstead and the moment we got there several people wanted to buy him; but there was no way, because we all had a feeling that he was going to be a little bit special. He then went out to jump a couple of clear rounds. Come July, my sister Mary went with him to a show in Bridgwater and for some reason he got tied up to the lorry with his bridle on and something frightened him which made him pull back and injure his jaw.'

A few days later David returned to Hickstead and prepared to jump him in ring two – not quite as imposing as the main arena but well laid out and fairly impressive. It was then that the horse did something his rider will never forget. They jumped three clear rounds in the class but, in order to go through the finish in the quickest way possible, David pulled him sharply on one side of the mouth and in doing so aggravated the bruised jaw.

'He completely locked up, went into the side of the arena and jumped the rails from a sideways position. I don't know how he did it but, if he had just touched those rails, we would have taken a crashing fall and probably been badly hurt. That has never happened to me before or since, and I was eliminated for leaving the ring.'

There is no doubt that the horse has been somewhat unlucky during his career, even though he has many victories to his credit. In those early days, Mary was riding him on their parents' farm when he fell with her jumping a 2 foot 6 inch fence. She finished up with a broken collar-bone. Shortly afterwards, David took him to Lincoln to qualify for the Foxhunters but finished second and then later tried him in a couple of hunter classes.

'Mrs Gibson, from Leicestershire, rode him at Timken and told me that he was one of the best horses she had ever sat on in her life. It is true that he's unbelievably smooth.

'In 1972 he won the King George V Gold Cup at Wembley and in his second year went to Dublin where they usually build very good courses. But on this occasion it was one of the biggest tracks built in Europe that year, for the Aga Khan Trophy. The good German mare Simona had a clear round and 4 faults, while my horse had 4 faults twice. They were the best two in the class and, when you think it was his first Nations Cup, and what Simona went on to do, it really was a first-class effort. But the thing was I wouldn't let him go to Hickstead beforehand because I thought the fences were going to be too big and here we were in Dublin jumping some with 7 foot spreads!'

That mammoth and highly courageous performance on the horse's part was, however, to take its toll, and it was to be a whole year before he fully recovered from his exertions. 'He had jumped brilliantly, but it was too much to have asked at that stage of his life. He was anxious in his own mind and took a long time to find his form again. At one stage I had seventeen seconds in succession and was beginning to get a little bit worried. But that run was broken in a class at Guildford.

'It was an incredible competition because Alan Oliver had gone clear on Sweep and then I had a faultless round with Sportsman to go into the jump-off. The course was altered and Alan was the first to go. But Sweep hit several of the fences and finished with a total of 16 faults. Then it was my turn and I didn't go very well but still managed to beat him after having 12 faults. How often do you see a horse winning with that number of mistakes in a jump-off?

'It was odd, really, because when he was being beaten during that long run of seconds, he was jumping some beautiful rounds, but just kept coming up against one that was better on the day. I know one thing now, though – that Guildford class taught me never to panic.'

It was a classic example of a rider not losing faith in his horse and David knew that, no matter how bad things were, the horse would eventually recover the form he'd shown before and during Dublin. His rider also learnt a good lesson that he has not forgotten: you must not expect too much too quickly and, if you ask the big question, sometimes the answer is not forthcoming. Also, because Sportsman has such a gentle nature and isn't prone to panicking himself, he was able to fight his way back and forget an experience that might have scarred him for life.

'He's an angel and such a sweetie. Even my vet says he is one of the most intelligent horses he has ever come across. Sportsman had to have an operation three years ago and, just as he was coming round from the anaesthetic, I spoke to him from the stable door and he actually put his ears forward, looked at me and then went back down again. I could talk about him in glowing terms for ever because he really is so lovely.'

It is good to hear such sentiments, because it goes to prove that, even though he is one of the best riders in the the world and a former individual world champion, David's horses mean a lot to him and are not just a means to an end. Too many people use and abuse their horses for the sake of money and fame, but David never has and never will.

I have watched him compete for many years and not once have I seen him strike a horse in anger. That is simply not his style – which is, perhaps, why he towers above many others in his profession. A typical example of his control came at the Towerlands show in 1980, when he rode Queensway's Sportsman in the £10,000 Rimas Challenge, organized and run by Lister Welch, his agent and a man who has done and will continue to do a lot for show jumping.

In this event, which then carried the biggest first-prize money in the world, David, Harvey Smith and Eddie Macken had the stage to themselves knowing that the winner would take all. It was a thrilling competition and David was going very well until Sportsman refused at one of the fences and dumped him on the floor. He has never done it before or since and, with so much money at stake, it would have been easy for the rider to have lost his temper and given him a couple of cracks with his whip. He didn't touch the horse, apart from stroking his neck on remounting to give him confidence.

David could very easily have damaged his back because when he fell he landed on one of the show jumping poles and must have been in considerable discomfort. It would have been easy, too, to have remounted and left the arena because at that time, with Macken – the eventual winner – in such cracking form, his chance of success had vanished.

Sportsman has played a major part in David's career and helped him, among other things, to win his fourth Lancia car at Park Farm in Middlesex; he then took him to his final victory in the European World Cup Volvo League qualifier at the Birmingham show. In the final placing of those European qualifiers, David finished with a total of 54 points to head the list above Austria's Hugo Simon, who had 37.

Tabac Original

Another of David's highly rated horses is Tabac Original, whom he bought at the Dublin Spring show in 1973 when he had made the journey out there to view another horse to add to his string.

'While I was looking at the one I had gone out to buy, another man came over and told me that he had a horse that he thought I would like. However, he was asking a lot of money and at the time I thought there was no way I was going to buy. But, after thinking about it, I realized that I hadn't even seen the horse move and to make up my mind so quickly was stupid.

'So the fellow pulled him out for me, told me

Tabac Original (previously Heatwave)

that he had won £80 to date and asked me if I would like to work him. When I got on him, I found that he didn't turn one way properly but did have a lovely jump in him – so careful and precise. When I had ridden him for a while, I told my father that I was interested and he agreed to do the negotiating. It took him twenty-four hours to buy the horse.

'He fails to be a Sportsman or Philco by about 3 inches in ability, but he is a superb horse – winning competitions both here and abroad even though he is just below top class. He's not a Grand Prix winner, although he has

won an awful lot of Grand Prix qualifiers. One of the great things about him is he is so fast against the clock. But he is, at the same time, very careful.

'You know, you learn as you go along in this job and I made a bad mistake by jumping Tabac one round too many on hard ground at the Three Counties once. He must have knocked himself because after that he went off completely and I was very worried about him. Just before I put him away, I took him to the Royal Highland show and for some unknown reason he cut his lip in the lorry.

'I called a vet who gave him an injection of penicillin and he seemed to have some sort of reaction to it. From that moment he wasn't worth the cost of a balloon. I don't know if it was all down to the drug but, what with that and the hard ground, he went right off for three months.

'This is one reason why I need so many horses in my string, so that I can afford to rest one and yet still keep on competing. It's such a long season now that I just have to have a certain number of horses available.'

David also revealed that Tabac Original, who was formerly known as Heatwave, is also very spooky and leaps about the place if he sees, or thinks he sees, something out of the ordinary.

'If I'm riding him around before a class and a worm pops its head up, I'll bet he'll see it. He's a lovely horse who just wants a bit of understanding and needs, above all, to be given confidence, because that is what he lacks. This is one of the ways he differs from Sportsman and Philco because they actually think they are kings and believe that I should treat them as such.

'In the past, Mister Softee was the same. I remember a classic example of this at Arena North, when Sportsman and Philco were lined up with Red Rum who, everyone will agree, is a king. Well my two stood alongside him during a presentation and you could see them weighing him up and sticking their chests out as though to say, "We're great as well, you know." Tabac Original just lacks that sort of confidence.'

David doesn't have to rely on records or notes to tell you about any of his horses; he knows them like friends and remembers with clarity everything about them. This is, perhaps, another reason they all seem to go so well for him. He understands exactly what they like and dislike and that is a great help when competing against strong opposition.

Queensway's Special

Another member of his string, Queensway's Special, was bought in Yorkshire in 1977 after his brother-in-law, Ted Edgar, phoned and

Queensway's Special (previously Forty Acres)

told him that the horse was available and the owners had agreed to bring it down from Yorkshire to Solihull for him to try. David, who had a French buyer lined up, had to tell Ted that the girl had changed her mind and couldn't make the trip from France. In order not to let Ted down, David agreed to go to Solihull anyway and ride the horse.

'I went there, not really knowing what to do, because I thought this French woman wanted me to buy her a horse. When she said she couldn't make it, I knew I couldn't just go and start throwing money about. I went to Solihull, rode him, and bought him right away. He's a lovely model of a horse and won two classes for me at Badminton one year. The only thing about him is that he always seems to start off slowly and needs a bit of work to make him flexible.

'When we went to Aachen in 1978, in preparation for the World Championships, I took him along as my second horse to Philco. I had talked with the selectors beforehand and they had agreed that I could use Philco exactly as I wanted. When we got there, after the warm-up class and two qualifiers, Philco – I thought – had done enough. I informed Ronnie Massarella, the chef d'équipe, that I would be riding Queensway's Special in the Nations Cup the following day and not Philco. There was all hell to pay. General Sir Cecil Blacker was there and we had all sorts of arguments, and I think it was lucky that it was all happening to me and not anyone else.

'In the end, even after Ronnie and I had rowed, Ronnie was the first to come up to me and say "Good luck lad" as I entered the arena.

'That's the sort of man he is and one of the reasons he is such a great team captain; even though you might have your ups and downs, he will still be in there punching for you.

'During the Nations Cup my horse jumped two clear rounds and you can imagine how I felt. It took the sting right out of the situation and Ronnie had a grin from ear to ear. He knew from that moment the feud was at an end.

'In fairness to all concerned, when I got back to Britain, General Blacker called me into his office to talk about it and gave me a mild dressing down. I would hate to think what would have happened if my horse hadn't jumped those two clear rounds.'

As it turned out, there had been very little danger of that, because Queensway's Special was in the best of form. So much so that Dutch television featured one of the rounds he had jumped in Aachen as being 'the best of the year'.

'He's only ever competed in one other Nations Cup and that was in Dublin when Sportsman wasn't going too well. I made a technical error between two of the fences and he knocked one down. So, in four rounds over Nations Cup fences, he has only had one fence down, which is not bad. He's a cocky sort of lad but very fast and beautiful to ride. He's also very kind in and out of the stable.'

Not all of David's horses are big and strapping with strides that seem to eat up the ground. He knows better than anyone else, perhaps, that it really doesn't matter if a jumper is not huge, as long as it is courageous and doesn't stop trying. It is quality and depth of character that really counts and, if a horse has ability, is looked after and ridden properly, he will eventually fulfil his promise.

Harris Home Care

'Harris Home Care, who used to be called Sunnyside Up, is a little chestnut horse whom I bought in 1978 about forty miles from my home. I had arranged to meet the person who was selling him at an indoor school where I was to try him out. I remember that it was a freezing cold day and the wind was blowing the wood shavings all over the place. They were about 9 inches deep in the school – far too deep on which to jump a horse. But he came in ridden by a young girl and proceeded to pop over a small jump. That was fine but after a while he started to get worse. But then I thought that even if I had had Philco with me, and had tried to jump him again and again in that deep going, he too would have tired.

Harris Home Care (previously Sunnyside Up)

'It transpired that the horse I was looking at had done two years eventing before turning to show jumping and had won a total of eleven classes and £250. Funnily enough, my father had seen him compete at Bicton and had marked him down as a possible buy for later in the season. In the end I bought him.

'The first show I ever took him to, Ted made me an offer for him but by that time I liked him too much to let him go and continued to ride him. In 1979 he jumped a total of nineteen consecutive clear rounds which more than justified the faith I had in him. Then we went to a show at Wandsworth where one of the classes comprised three rounds and the winner's prize was a mini car. Many people thought that my horse was too young at the time to have any chance, but he went in and won it for me.

'As far as character is concerned, he is a very nervous animal and, of all things, you mustn't take too much notice of him.'

There have been moments when David couldn't even get up on him, and it wasn't until his groom, Tina, told him how to handle the horse that he overcame the odd behaviour. Things came to a head when he went to mount

the horse one day in their indoor school.

'He was being one on the most awkward critters you can imagine and I was getting well and truly fed up. But then Tina came over to me and said, "Don't take any notice of him. Just walk straight up and tell him to stand still. Then get on. Don't, whatever you do, pamper him."

'Well I did just that and it worked to perfection and now I know exactly what to do with the little feller when he's mucking about.'

Pikant

Another horse that very few members of the public know about yet is one called Pikant. David bought him in 1979; he thinks he has a great future and will eventually rival the best in his yard.

'He's a German bred and I hope will turn out to be very good indeed.'

Then there is Mr Ross, bought by Phil Harris, who should also prove his worth.

Pikant

2 Highlights of My Life

The finest accolade a sports personality can receive is to be honoured by Her Majesty the Queen. It is something rather special in anyone's life and an occasion which is never forgotten. David received an OBE in 1970.

'I knew about it at the back end of 1969 after getting a letter from the Palace, but was asked to keep the news confidential until they had announced it in the New Year's Honours list.

My parents were thrilled and very proud that I was given the OBE, but I never use it on letterheads and things like that. I feel that people know that I have it and I don't really want to ram it down their throats. I would hate them to think that I am being big-headed.

Early days – David Broome with his trophies

'I believe the British Equestrian Federation must have nominated me for it, which was very flattering. And I'll never forget the day we set off, dolled up in our morning suits to go to the Palace. My mother and father were with me and when we arrived it was really fantastic. Then I saw about 350 other people there for the same reason and it put it all in perspective.

'After I had been given the award, we had to dash off back to Wembley because I was riding in a class that afternoon at the Royal International. As we were hot-rodding away, I took a wrong turn and arrived at the Empire Pool later than I should have done, but the judges were marvellous. They knew where I had been and allowed me to go last in the competition, so I had time to change from morning dress into breeches and boots. Then it seemed that luck was with me, because I went out and shared equal first with Marion Mould.'

I asked David if, after the OBE and the win at Wembley, he went out on the town to celebrate such a remarkable day. The answer was somewhat surprising.

David Broome at BBC Television's Sports Personality of the Year Awards 1960, with Peter Dimmock and Peter Wilson

'We're not a big family for that sort of thing – as my wife will confirm – and we never show a lot of emotion. I am inclined to treat every day the same and that is where, perhaps, I tend to miss out on life. I have been lucky enough to have had so many good times during my career that the really special ones don't seem to register. I would hate to appear blasé about it all, but the thing is I never have ups or downs because I am a very constant person. Sometimes people can get the wrong idea about me because of it. When my wife prepares a superb meal for me I might just tell her it is good – which, when she has spent four hours cooking it, is not an awful lot of praise. Fortunately, she understands me.'

One of the best moments of David's career came very early on in his life when he was picked to represent Britain abroad for the first time. He was just nineteen, with the world at his feet and looking forward to making his mark in show jumping.

'I could have gone in 1958 when Sir Harry Llewellyn, who has been one of my great mentors, gave me the chance to ride at Dublin. But my father quite rightly told him that I was not ready and to wait a year.

'Twelve months later, true to his word, my father said I could compete outside Britain, and it was great, although to start with things didn't go too well. On the way to Harwich to catch the boat, our lorry was involved in an accident. We tried to go under a 10 foot 3 inch bridge with a horsebox which was over 11 feet high.

'The lorry had wooden uprights and as we went through the bridge sheered the top right off it. We had two horses inside. Luckily one just had a broken headcollar, while the other slightly cut his face. Then, while we were getting the ramp down to unload them, a train went over the bridge. But the horses didn't bat an eyelid and we eventually got a contractor to take us to Harwich. We made it just in time to board the boat. Still, things came right in the end because I won the first class I ever took part in abroad.'

Was he upset that his father had not allowed him to go to that Dublin show the year before?

'Not at all. One only heard then of the occasional team going abroad and people, particularly show jumpers, didn't seem to travel very much anyway. These days it is all very different, and a sixteen-year-old who has won a £20 open class thinks he has a right to go overseas. In 1958 my horse was a leading money winner and yet my father considered that I was only half ready and he was correct. I have always been of the firm opinion that a rider must earn the right to represent his country. As far as my own father was concerned, it wasn't just a case of taking part. If we couldn't go out and win, there wasn't any point in going.'

Throughout David's life his father Fred has played a major part in his career and has always been on hand to offer advice and help when it has been asked for or needed. In 1970, when his son won the individual World Championship he was once again by his side.

'The thing that made me qualify and drove me on was the fact that my old friend and rival Harvey Smith had qualified. That got me going because he was cock-a-hoop over winning the first two classes. I was way down the line and realized that I had an enormous challenge in front of me, so I decided I had better start thinking very seriously about the job in hand. On the third day the old spirit came back and I went out and jumped two clear rounds to qualify on Beethoven. And I

Hickstead 1968 on Beethoven – the horse he rode at the 1970 World Championships at La Baule

think, from that moment, I had half defeated the others. They all thought that Beethoven was difficult to ride, although brilliant, and it seemed to put the fear of God into them.

'The worst thing about that championship was the two-day wait between qualifying and the final. They were sleepless nights for me because I just kept on wondering if I would win the title and that thought was forever churning over in my mind.

'Although many of the other people were getting a bit uptight, my father worked Beethoven on the morning of the final as if it was just another competition. Some were changing bridles and doing all sorts of things to give them an edge, but father just remained totally cool and tried to keep everything normal. His ability and backing was one of the keys to my success.

'During the final session each of the riders had to ride the others' horses and, when my turn came for Donald Rex, who had been ridden by Alwin Schockemohle, I had already jumped three clear rounds and was just ahead of the Italian, Graziano Mancinelli. I took Donald Rex into the practice area and Ted Edgar was there with my father. Ted's a great man to have around when there is a battle on but the first thing he did was to give me a rollicking. I had just ridden three difficult horses and he thought I was going to sleep.

'In fact, I was the only rider to have a fence down on that particular horse and that happened about three from home. After that I had to turn into a loop and then come out and jump a large vertical. As we neared the fence, I almost hooked his back teeth out, but he measured it perfectly and cleared the fence easily. Then I got a good stride going into the last – the water – and he went about 9 feet in the air and landed as far out the other side. And it

David Broome riding Donald Rex to victory and the 1970 World Championship title

Mister Softee's last great performance made David European Champion for the third time. Hickstead 1969

was while we were going over that that my excitement at winning came and I remember saying to myself at the time, "That will do it".'

Apart from the world title, David has also won three European Championships and the one that sticks out in his mind was the third title he won on Mister Softee at Hickstead in Sussex in 1969.

'That was great. In those days the winner of the final class took all, and every rider went in knowing that they had to finish first in that particular class to succeed in becoming the European champion. It could have been 'anybody's at the time but Mister Softee jumped out of his mind and it was, in fact, his last great performance.'

To hold a record in any sport gives the participant a great deal of pleasure. David is the only rider to have won four King George V Gold Cups.

David won the King George V Gold Cup for the first time in 1960 on Sunsalve – he went on to win it three more times

'I had the first wrapped up in 1960 on Sunsalve, but I didn't realize at the time how important the competition really was until I had the cup on my sideboard for twelve months. It's gold and has St George on his horse spearing the dragon, and even in the early sixties I think it was insured for about £10,000. It really is beautiful.

'When Sunsalve won, I was also second on Wildfire and it was only the second time that I had ever ridden in the class. Then, in 1966, I won it again on Mister Softee who jumped the only two clear rounds, and in 1972 I took it with Sportsman who has always, as you know, been one of my favourite horses. Five years later Philco won it for me at the same time as my sister Liz won the Queen Elizabeth Cup on Everest Wallaby. That really was a show to remember.'

The name David Broome appears with regularity in the record books and this is something of which he is justifiably proud. To ride is all very well, but to win major championships is altogether a different story.

'If one spends twenty-five years show jumping, there wants to be something which stands up to scrutiny for all time. Just to take part for all those years and not actually do anything would, to me, be completely meaningless. I have been lucky. I find winning money important, but at the same time I realize that when people do look back on my record they will see that I have achieved something – and that means a lot to me.'

The year before David won that record King George V Gold Cup, he married Graham Fletcher's sister at Thirsk, in Yorkshire. It was 4 May.

'I looked at the show jumping calendar and saw there was a show on the 9th. My poor unsuspecting wife had no idea that, after our honeymoon in Scotland, I would be competing at that show on the way back. Before the wedding, however, the jitters set in and I have

never experienced anything like it in my life. My wedding speech was the most diabolical one you ever heard and it was simply because of nerves. If someone went into a show jumping ring the way I felt then, they wouldn't have had a prayer.'

David's wife is, of course, no stranger to show jumping and used to ride ponies in competition. Later she graduated to horses but now no longer competes. She is intelligent, extremely good looking and can hold conversations on innumerable subjects. Did it help at all that she didn't compete any more?

'I would say that only about 3 per cent of the conversation in our house is about horses and that keeps me sane. Liz understands the job and what it's all about but we very rarely talk about horses or show jumping. I should think that very few other riders are so lucky, because their wives compete and, of course, the sport must always be discussed at length.

'I first met Liz when she was eighteen at a little show in Lancashire when she turned up with her brother Graham. During the afternoon my groom asked if she would hold one of my horses, which she did, and it wasn't until much later that I learnt he had offered her 2s. for doing so. I always thought she was very good looking and kept telling Graham that he had a smashing sister. I eventually asked her to go out with me and we courted for six months and then married. It was the best move I ever made.'

Does he mind his family being at shows with him?

'No, not at all, but I do have a dreadful habit of ignoring them. I get so involved with the horses and what I am going to do that they seem to lose out. I feel very guilty about it because I sometimes ignore Liz when I shouldn't.'

David and Liz have a son – James – and the question many people have asked is: knowing how hard it has all been and how tough it is to reach and stay at the top, would David like him to take up show jumping one day?

'I think for purely selfish reasons I would love him to be a show jumper, because I would

like him to be good at it so that I could be one proud dad. He has a pony of his own at the moment but, instead of riding it, he just loves to walk it around on a lead rein.'

Would he and Liz like to have more children? It was a question he answered immediately.

'I think if we only have James, he will finish up being terribly spoilt and I don't think that would be right or fair on him or anyone else. So I think we will have another child.'

Because he is always dashing from one end of the country to the other, David has installed a radio phone in his horsebox, so he can keep in constant touch with his wife and child when he is away riding. On many showgrounds there is not always easy access to a telephone – which means that Liz cannot always be contacted as much as David would like.

'I thought the only way to solve the problem was to buy a mobile phone which I could use in the lorry and in my car. It has a magnetic aerial which I just fix into the roof. I have had a great many things in my life, but this is one of the most pleasant. When I first used it while driving along the motorway I got a great kick out of it. Now, no matter where I am, I can always pick up the phone to speak to Liz. This means that she knows when and where I will be at any given moment.'

James helps in the stable

39

3 Sisters Mary and Liz

No athlete or rider can reach the heights of stardom without a lot of help from those around him because the long, hard road to the top is peppered with hidden hazards. Seb Coe has strong support from his father and David can call upon every member of his family at Mount Ballan Manor in Gwent.

One of those who has his interests very much at heart is his sister Mary who, among many other things, supervises the stables, the feeding and the buying of tack. She is a woman who understands exactly what is required to keep the show on the road, and the contribution she makes is much appreciated by her brother.

'She has some very nice ideas about riding and will sit on the horses for hours, larking about with them and getting them in the right frame of mind. I'm afraid I haven't got the patience for that and hate riding at home

David, Philco and sister Mary at home in the stable yard

Mary Broome hunting with the Curre on Let's Go

because I've always got so much else to do.

'Mary just goes about her work quietly and can be relied upon to do just about anything that is required. I don't say we work in perfect harmony all the time, because like any brother and sister we have our moments of aggro – but it always comes out right in the end.

'She was a great help to me when Queensway's Big Q first came to the yard and I just couldn't get anywhere with him. As I have said, he had taken seventeen days to arrive from the man we bought him from, and I didn't bother to give him that much work before taking him to Badminton. With hindsight, it was a mistake on my part but, as we had adopted the same plan with Philco a few years

earlier, I was under the impression that all would be well.

'Philco had gone to the Badminton show and had performed like a champion, jumping two rounds and going clear in both. Everyone could see what a good horse he was and I really thought it would be the same with Queensway's Big Q. So I rode him on the Thursday, gave him a pop over a couple of fences the following day and set off for Badminton.

'I knew that his owner, Phil Harris, was rather excited about the horse and was going to Badminton with very high hopes. He couldn't have been more disappointed: Queensway's Big Q went like an absolute drain and was much too fresh. Knowing what I do now about the horse, I realize I was totally wrong and that it had been a suicide trip from the very start. After we had jumped the water, I pulled him up but the people who were watching didn't know that I had done so because I couldn't hold one side of him.

'I was terribly despondent and thought, at the time, that he was going to be nothing but trouble. As I had other horses to ride, I asked Mary to take him over and said that she could have him for a few months. I was very lucky to be able to do that, because I knew only too well that he would be in good hands with Mary.

'Poor Phil felt sick. He had just paid a lot of money for the horse and there we were making a mess of things. He wouldn't even jump a practice fence properly and, every time Phil put one up, Queensway's Big Q would proceed to knock it down. I think that happened about five times, which didn't please any of us. But Mary worked on him for a few months and he got better and better.

'She doesn't rush horses at all, and as she weighs a lot less than me she can spend hours on their backs. They love it and eventually come round to her way of thinking.'

But, like all horsemen and women, Mary Broome has had her fair share of the hard times and has, on occasions, been hurt when riding or schooling the horses in her charge. When Sportsman first arrived at the Broome stables, Mary took a terrible crash from him over a stile and ended up with a broken collar-bone. The horse, too, was somewhat unlucky and hurt his chest.

It does, however, take a lot more than that to stop her and within a short time she was back in the saddle and working harder than ever.

'She has her own interests as well where show jumping is concerned and has ridden in the Ladies' National Championships at Royal Windsor. But nowadays she doesn't get a lot of time. I think she would still like to ride in the Queen Elizabeth II Cup at Wembley, though.

'I have had a lot of help from my parents and my other sister, Liz, who is married to Ted Edgar. When Liz was at home she used to do an awful lot of work and, when she married, and

left, it was amazing how many people thought I would start going downhill and that it would be the beginning of the end. But it wasn't – life goes on, and that's what it's all about. I will admit, though, that the gap left by Liz would be difficult to fill without Mary.

'Liz, of course, is happy and doing very well in show jumping. But, although we are in different camps and ride a lot against each other, we often talk and discuss horses. She knows that whatever I say is mostly in confidence and if I ask for her advice I know I will always get it. And, of course, the reverse is true.

'And Ted is one of my great friends at shows because I know that whatever he tells me will be the truth. There are no half-measures with the man and that is what I like about him. He's been in show jumping for a long time, knows the game backwards and is a great person to rely on.'

The Broomes and the Edgars are two of the biggest family names in show jumping and, although David and his family live in Gwent, and Liz and Ted in Warwickshire, they often go and stay with each other and discuss various aspects of show jumping. David also knows that, if he wants to stable horses for the night at Ted's yard, all he has to do is to take them there. The same, of course, goes for Ted with David's yard. Also, Ted and Liz not only produce some very good horses for Everest Double Glazing, but also they have brought along one of the best young riders in the country – Nick Skelton.

In a very short time this talented young man has won many major competitions, including the Junior European Show Jumping Championship, and he is, in fact, the holder of the British high jump record. Both Liz and Ted have given him every chance and he has more than proved that he was worth the time and effort. He travels all over the world with them and it wouldn't surprise those who know

Ted Edgar in action

Nick Skelton, Liz and Ted Edgar's protégé and one of the best young riders in the country

anything about show jumping to see him, one day, taking David's place at the top of the league.

The support and help that Mary gives David at home leaves him free to concentrate on the other important aspects of his life, which include running a carpet business with his brother Frederick, who was a very good show jumping rider until turning to the world of commerce.

'We have the carpet shops, and at home we have the farm to run and, when I think about it, I suppose horses come about third down the list. That is why it is so nice to have people around me who will help out when it's required.'

This is, perhaps, one of the answers to his astounding success in the saddle: without the worry of what's happening back at the stables, he can concentrate on what he is going to do when he arrives at a show. One of his greatest assets is being able to relax totally, even when time is at a premium, or the pressure is on and is mounting rapidly. This was very much in evidence at the Badminton show last year when he was riding in the Whitbread Show Jumping Trophy.

The class started at 4.30 but David was nowhere to be seen thirty minutes before the event. He had been walking around the trade stands with his wife and turned up just in time to have a quick cup of coffee and then beat the hell out of the opposition.

'Pressure never seems to worry me and I know as far as that is concerned I am very fortunate. I don't mind the travelling, either, because I happen to enjoy what I do. Many riders go away from show jumping to take a holiday, but I would much rather take my holiday at the shows. Because of my other business interests I suppose I am nearly always fresh when it comes to the actual riding of horses and that helps.'

Over the years, through talent, hard work and determination, David has become a household name and knows exactly how important it is to take full notice of his fans – and there are, indeed, thousands of them. No matter how busy he is, he will go out of his way to satisfy the hungry demands of the youngsters who clamour for his autograph. He is happy that they ask, and they are overjoyed when they can walk away with the name 'David Broome' written across a page of their treasured autograph books. He is their idol and he is well aware that he has a responsibility to them.

Public interest, however, can be overwhelming at times: at outdoor shows, when the horsebox is parked near the arena, people flock to it in order to see his horses and just look at them standing between the partitions.

My younger daughter has a picture of Philco when he first arrived in this country. That was many years ago, but the shot still has pride of place in her album and she will never forget the day she was allowed to stroke his neck. If I remember correctly, she didn't wash that hand for two days. As far as the young people are concerned, that is what heroes are for: to worship and to hold dear. David realizes this and goes out of his way to accommodate them.

4 The Friends I Have Made

Any great sportsman meets thousands of people during his career; many are fans, some hangers-on and a few, just a few, are classed as real friends. David's sister Liz comes highest on his list of those he can turn to when necessary.

'She is always at the shows and prepared to listen. I don't say I go and cry on her shoulder if things go wrong because I don't behave like that, but it's always good to know that, if I do need to discuss one or two things, she is there. The same goes for Ted. They are good friends as well as being part of the family, and the combination of these factors makes the bond between us very strong. I can also count on Graham Fletcher, my wife's brother. We get on very well and I think he is a highly accomplished rider. We have much in common and always have a lot of fun when we meet up at the shows.'

Whenever anyone thinks of show jumping, they automatically link the names of David Broome and Harvey Smith because they are two of the present-day greats and they have brought the sport into the public eye and kept it there. What does David think of his famous rival and friend?

Graham Fletcher with Easy Rider and Clare Glen

Harvey Smith never gives up and David says that this competitive spirit has done more for him as a rider than anything else

'I have known "Smudger" for a great many years and, although he probably doesn't know it, he has done more for me as a rider than anyone else. And the reason for that is that he never stops trying to win and that has brought the best out in me because I have had to try and keep on beating him. A rider at top level needs competition and Harvey has consistently provided it all the years I have known him. His great quality is that he never gives up and I think that has kept us both going.

'Another rider who has done very well in recent years is Eddie Macken. He and Boomerang were brilliant and together won a great many classes, including, of course, four British Jumping Derbys. Nobody has ever done that before and I was very sorry to learn that Boomerang had cracked a bone in one of his feet and has now retired. Having a brilliant horse makes a great deal of difference to any rider.

'Derek Ricketts is also a man I like very much and, although a lot of people wouldn't know it, I am always ready to listen to what he has to say because he does talk a lot of sense. He has worked his way to the top and can be proud of what he has achieved.'

When a person like David is left out of a Nations Cup team one would expect him to feel somewhat disenchanted with the man who made the decision. At Hickstead's May meeting last year Ronnie Massarella did just that, even though David was his number one rider. At that time Philco was suffering from an allergy and wasn't available for the big occasion, so David was left out of the squad. We were recording this chapter at Hickstead and I asked him what he thought of Massarella.

'He's one of the best there is and being dropped was just one of those things. It can

Ronnie Massarella with the successful 1979 European Championships team. Left to right: *Caroline Bradley, Malcolm Pyrah, Derek Ricketts, Ronnie Massarella, David Broome*

Top riders in pensive mood. Left to right: *Lionel Dunning, David Broome, Harvey Smith, Graham Fletcher*

happen to anyone at any time and has to be accepted. Ronnie puts the team before the individual and, once he has decided, that's it. You only have to look at his record to see that he is more often right than wrong and, at the end of the day, that's what matters. Certainly it can be disappointing when you're left out of a British team but the only thing to do is to keep on trying to get back on it.'

When Massarella made that decision and left David as a spectator he, too, was concerned and maybe a little anxious. If his team of riders, consisting of David's sister Liz, Lionel Dunning, Robert Smith and John Whitaker, hadn't triumphed he would have set himself up to be shot at. He explained how he felt. 'I was very sad because David had done so much for us. But the other riders' horses had been going so well that I had to give them their chance. Leaving him out, though, did hurt.'

David, however, did have some compensation because Liz Edgar, who hadn't at that time ridden in a Nations Cup for sixteen years, jumped two superb clear rounds on Forever and so helped keep things in the family. It was right, too, that she was given the opportunity.

Two top riders missing at that Lambert & Butler meeting were West German Paul Schockemohle and Austria's Hugo Simon. Both come high on David's list.

'Paul is so dedicated it's hard to believe, and I would think he jumps at least twice as

many fences as I do during a year, because when he is not actually competing he spends hours schooling. He's a perfectionist and deserves all he gets because he works so hard. Paul has also done a lot for the International Riders Club and we all have a lot to thank him for. He has certainly got me thinking on the right lines as far as that is concerned.

'Hugo is a man who always looks and is happy, and he is desperately hard to beat. When he and his horse Gladstone get going it is almost impossible for anyone to get near them. They are a formidable combination.'

Show jumping is one of the few sports where women can compete on equal terms with men and one of those who has emerged and won the hearts of all is Caroline Bradley.

'Caroline is superb, dedicated and highly talented, and anything she gets out of show jumping she deserves. Anyone will tell you that she is a credit to the sport and will be around for a long time to come.'

Apart from the riders, does he have much time for those involved in the administration of show jumping and what, for instance, does he think of General Sir Cecil Blacker, one of the association's top men?

'Firstly, he is a very straight man who is completely and utterly above board, and he appreciates the riders' problems. He has also done a lot of fund raising and made sure that we have all done better than in the past. I think that, without him, much less would have been achieved as far as we are concerned. Most people tended to take the view that, because we have been riding for several years, there was no earthly reason why we shouldn't carry on in the same old way.

'In his time General Blacker has come up against a lot of opposition. I suppose this might have been the result of jealousy on the part of some people who may have thought he was a bit of an upstart who happened to get things done. They have no reason to be jealous, however, because they have been doing a good job over the years collecting money, and without them we couldn't manage. But some of them *were* jealous, I am sure, and it was all rather sad really.

'That is not the reason he announced at the Federation's Annual General Meeting in London his intention of retiring. He did that to comply with the rules and could, if he had the desire to do so, return in two years' time.'

At that meeting, General Blacker also nominated the Duke of Wellington as his replacement. The nomination met with approval.

During his time in show jumping, David has been in contact with many people who work for television and radio including Dorian Williams, equestrian commentator, author, and chairman of the British Horse Society. Williams has made a major contribution to show jumping and is one of the finest commentators in the world.

'He's still probably the best in the world at putting enthusiasm and drama into a show jumping commentary. Somehow he seemed to get it across so much better than the others and I take my hat off to him because he injected so much excitement into what he was doing.'

What then does he think of Raymond Brooks-Ward, who also commentates for the BBC and is managing director of British Equestrian Promotions?

'I've known Raymond for some twenty years or more and he tells me that I was the subject of his first interview – at the Rome Olympics, in 1960. We have always got along very well and, as well as his broadcasting, he is a good show organizer.'

One of show jumping's great characters is George Hobbs, a former top international rider and now a man who heads the sport's Rules Committee.

'He would always give riders sound advice, even if they were competing against him. And, more often than not, his own advice would beat

him, but he never did mind as long as he was helping someone. He's one of the good guys, totally genuine and plays a very important role on the executive committee. He is the underdogs' champion.

'George and I have had some hellish rows – absolute ding dongs – but we are the best of friends. He believes he represents the total membership of the BSJA, while I only represent the top eight, and for those reasons we have constant battles. I admire him greatly because we need men like him.'

Having discussed some of the administrators, we moved on to show organizers and a man who turned a field into one of the best show jumping arenas in the world. His name – Douglas Bunn.

'He and I have had as many rows as two people can have but we always remain friends. In fact, he is a man I respect. At one of his meetings Duggie had put a new ditch on the course and the idea was, in my opinion, absolutely crackers because the fence that was built over it was enormous. At 10.30 a.m. it did

Douglas Bunn. Despite many disagreements, he and David remain the best of friends

tend to smack you in the eyes, and at first we all raised hell about it and several of us refused to jump in the class.

'I find Douglas very stubborn and, when he sticks his chin out, he really sticks it out, and the only answer is not to jump. Anyway, we both finished up being interviewed by David Vine on television. I said what I thought and then Douglas gave his view and, I might add, there was no mincing of words. But the funny thing was that, the very same evening, I needed to borrow a car to go and see my sponsor at Orpington, and the only man who had a vehicle available was Duggie. So off I went to ask him if I could have a loan of it; he said that it was all right but I had to go to the cook, up at his house, and collect the keys from her. When I eventually found her, she gave me the biggest slagging under the sun for being nasty to her master on television.

'Douglas and I have had some really hard rows but he never holds a grudge and that is one of his greatest virtues.

'I think Hickstead has got better over the years because the spread fences are nowhere near as wide as they used to be. You can take a very good horse down there and jump him safely. The prize money is excellent but the only criticism I have – and that's a temporary one – is that you are not allowed to ride more than one horse in the main class.'

A few years ago I wrote several stories calling upon show organizers to pay the top riders stabling fees at major meetings which were sponsored and televised. I have often wondered if it did any good.

'Our stabling fees were paid in 1979 because some of the organizers entered into the spirit of the thing. But, in my view, it should depend on the status of the show and if we are talking, for argument's sake, about a major county show, then I have very definite views about it. We sometimes put on the entertainment in the main ring for more than an hour and if we do

David Broome wins the British Jumping Derby at Hickstead 1966 on Mister Softee

not win or get placed we are basically doing it for nothing. But we might be followed by other entertainment, which has been paid for. So why shouldn't we just get something like free stabling?

'Now at the Wales and West show, which my father organizes, we don't get enough people through the gate to justify giving riders anything – and we don't make any money ourselves. In fact, I think the riders are lucky to have a show like ours to come to because the novices they jump in rings four or five are not entertaining anyone but they are gaining valuable experience.'

His views on shows which are heavily sponsored and attract television are clear and he considers that some riders should be paid appearance money.

'That's absolutely right because many of the shows are sold on the fact that the top riders are competing. If you took away the best twelve from places like Birmingham, Olympia and Wembley, I am certain that in the end public interest would die, because over the years each rider has amassed his or her own group of fans. Take Eddie Macken or Harvey Smith – they have a fantastic following, and I have my Welsh fans: they come along to support us, just as much as going to watch the sport. I'm certain that if the top dozen riders went missing, interest would disappear with them.'

That apart, one certain way of causing the death of show jumping as we know it would be the withdrawal of sponsorship money. A situation of which David is very well aware.

'I need a sponsor in order to survive – there is no question about that. Having made that clear, however, the sport also needs it for the prize money. That is why, if a class is sponsored and being televised, everyone concerned must make sure that those who are putting up the money get a fair crack of the whip. They must be seen to be getting it, too, because they are vital to the sport. Keeping the right balance is important, as well; that is why you never see me or Harvey Smith, for example, hogging the limelight.'

Opposite: *David Broome on Manhattan coming down the famous Derby Bank at Hickstead, 1971*

Above: *David Broome on Queensway's Sportsman at the 1980 Birmingham show – the 1981 World Cup venue*

Was there, I asked, anything he particularly disliked at the major shows he attended last year?

'At the Bath and West a lot of humble pie was eaten on my part during and after the Babycham Gold Cup, won by Robert Smith. I must say that it was a very good class but when I walked the course I thought it was enormous and some of the other riders agreed.

'Normally when this has happened in the past we have usually had a word with the course builder, told the judges, or just rubbed out our numbers from the starters' board. Then something has been done. In this instance I withdrew and afterwards one of the fences was altered, but not the crucial one.

'When the class started the course seemed to jump better than it had walked and, the more I sat there watching, the more I realized I wasn't going to win any money. So, having declared myself a competitor an hour before the class, there was nothing in the rule book to say I had to do anything before going into the ring, even though I had withdrawn. I swallowed my pride and asked the judges if I could start in the class. I was three or four from the end and so hadn't missed my turn. But they refused to let me go and I got rather heated because as a professional I think I am entitled to a good decision.'

In fact, the show didn't turn out well for him at all, because disaster struck with a vengeance and he lost Manhattan when the horse collapsed and died suddenly of a heart attack in the collecting ring.

'It was horrible but I do firmly believe that was the way he wanted to go when his time was up. It happened very quickly and there was no chance that he suffered. One minute we were standing up and the next he was lying dead. One of my legs was trapped underneath him and I was helped out by some of the other riders, but I was only bruised. I think Manhattan was dead before he hit the ground. He was an all-rounder and I miss him. He was eighteen years old and a great friend.'

At the beginning of the season, David rode in the Rimas Challenge at Towerlands in Essex. As mentioned earlier, it was a unique competition, devised on that occasion by his agent, Lister Welch. The winner took all and those involved were David, Harvey Smith and Ireland's Eddie Macken.

'I think as a one-off it got people thinking differently and it was the first out-of-the-ordinary thing that had happened in show jumping for a long time. Up until then the sport was in danger of getting itself into a rut. With hindsight, it would probably have been better if it had been open to more people. But I think the fans enjoyed it and I feel sure the sponsor was given value for money.'

As it was then the biggest first prize in the world some people might have thought that the riders were in a position to split the prize money so that nobody went away empty handed. That, however, did not happen.

'I suppose there will always be those who think along those lines but Eddie won the money and that's a fact.'

Eddie Macken won the Rimas Challenge at Towerlands in 1979 and collected what was then the biggest first prize in the world

57

5 A Question of Time

Riding against the clock is one of the main reasons show jumping has caught on in a big way with the public, because seeing a close finish at Wembley or Olympia can be as exciting as backing a horse who wins the Derby by a short head. I mention those two venues because they are staged indoors, heavily televised and, with expert cameramen at work, the public can sometimes feel they are actually in the saddle with the rider as he gallops to the finishing line.

David is one of those competitors who very rarely appear to be going fast in speed classes, even though when the results are known he has often clipped one, or even two seconds off the leader's time. People have actually asked me how he does it.

David never appears to be going very fast when riding against the clock but often cuts seconds off the leader's time; here he is riding Sportsman to victory in the Daily Telegraph Cup at the Horse of the Year Show, Wembley, 1976

'I find that very interesting and can only assume that, when everything goes right for me it looks easy. But the fact is it's really just a matter of cutting corners and meeting each fence right. That saves a lot of time. But I never practise for speed at home because I firmly believe that, if a horse is schooled properly at the start of his career, you are halfway to winning the battle.

'Another thing I always do is walk the course before riding it, and study the course plan. This is a must because a rider can lose valuable seconds if he isn't sure where he should be going. But I never pace out the distances before each fence if they are obviously more than four of my horse's strides apart. To me, the mathematics of it all doesn't matter in those cases, and you just use your eye to get the stride right. I will always remember a time I did just keep on counting, way past the eight strides and, when I asked my horse to take off where I thought he should, I ended up on the floor. It was a lesson well learnt.

'The fans often see riders striding around the ring, pacing out the distances, but I can never understand those who actually take it to extremes and walk round the bends. There is absolutely no need for that because it is meaningless. How can you possibly pace out a bend?

'I find one of the hardest men to beat in speed classes is Harvey Smith. He is brilliant at judging pace and turning sharply into the fences, even if it sometimes looks as though he is coming in at too much of an angle. But he knows exactly what he is doing at all times and when he goes clear it is often a very hard job to catch him.

'The draw makes a big difference, too, because the one who is going last always has an edge over the others. By the time it gets round to his turn to compete, he knows exactly what he has to beat. I have won plenty of classes going first, but it's always best to be going near the end.

'Perhaps the people who have the hardest job are the course builders, who sometimes have only minutes to rebuild the fences. I have had arguments with them before now, but on

Walking the course before the competition can save vital seconds in a jump-off against the clock

the whole they are a good bunch. It is in everyone's interests to have the fences built properly and the distances in between them right. In fact, some of the complaints I have made have been because the course has been too easy. Small fences can sometimes make the course builders look silly, particularly when you have a mass of riders going clear. In such cases the classes go well over time and everyone runs late.'

David has ridden all over the world but when asked what are his favourite shows he mentions Dublin, Wembley and Olympia.

'Olympia is rather special because it's held near Christmas time when everybody is happy. It also means, of course, that the season is at an end and we can all go off for a short rest before

Harvey Smith, brilliant at judging pace and turning sharply, is one of the hardest riders to beat in speed classes. Here riding Speakeasy at the Wales and West Show

starting again. I don't think I have any favourite shows as such and nowadays I tend to pick and choose were I want to go. It's very nice to be in that position because it means I'm not dashing from one end of the country to the other.'

One thing David does think very deeply about is the future of show jumping and he believes the organizers must be extremely careful to avoid overexposure of the sport.

'There is no doubt television has helped make show jumping, but it does seem that an awful lot of it is being put on nowadays. And, I

would imagine, if you are not a dedicated fan but on the borderline, you might tend to feel that it was being pushed at you. That might just put some people off because many of them would prefer to be able to have a choice of viewing. It hasn't reached a crucial stage yet – but I feel that it might not be too far away.'

I asked him what changes he has seen during his many years in the sport.

'One of the most notable changes is the fact that show jumping has grown into a major spectator sport, but I do not agree with those who think there are too many fixtures. It simply means a rider can be selective and, if he plans his season properly, his horses are not overworked or jumped too much. I am a great believer in bringing horses along slowly and giving them plenty of time to gain experience because that way they last a lot longer and should, anyway, be treated with respect. My idea is always to think in the long term and keep my horses for as long as I possibly can. My philosophy is: if you look after them, they will look after you . . . . It's as simple as that.'

I put it to him that he might be stretched to explain what his ambition is after being so constantly successful. He didn't think twice about the question.

'Certainly I have been very lucky and have experienced the good times in show jumping, but what I like doing is taking my horses right through the grades – from Grade C to Grade A. That gives me a great deal of pleasure and satisfaction because, if they do become very good, I know I have played a major part in their success. But none of these things can happen overnight and, because it takes time, it is a challenge and an ambition to get everything right.'

It is always interesting to know whether, if a great sportsman had his time over again, he would change it in any way or start again in his chosen field. Some, with the benefit of hindsight, might suggest there were easier and less painful ways of making a living then being a top show jumper.

'I wouldn't change anything because I love show jumping and the sport has done a lot for me. I have taken out much more than I have put in and that is why I try to help others whenever I possibly can in the sport. It owes me nothing and, if I had the chance to do it all over again, I would.

'That is why I find it so interesting watching the young riders now because they have very bright futures, particularly people like Robert Smith, Nick Skelton and Michael Whitaker. There are others, but the three I have mentioned have proved that they have a lot of natural talent.'

Even the thought that those same people, now young and extremely talented, might knock him out of pole position doesn't worry the former world champion.

'Not at all. Having these youngsters around makes life much more interesting and keeps us all on our toes. It is always good to see them win because at their age they need encouragement and winning is the best thing for them. But they all work very hard and deserve to succeed.'

Hundreds of thousands of young people watch show jumping throughout the year in Britain: would he recommend that some of them try to follow in his footsteps?

'I know for a fact that many of them would love to become show jumpers and I wouldn't like to discourage them in any way. But their dreams are unlikely to come to anything unless they have the backing in terms of both money and experience. Without the right environment they would have little chance at all and would just have to keep on dreaming. Most of us in show jumping have parents with farms, or families who are connected with horses in some way. We also have sponsorship and without it there is very little hope of people making the grade. I don't say they shouldn't try but would merely like to point out the pitfalls before they start.'

6 Phil Harris - Sponsor and Friend

At thirty-eight Phil Harris moves with the speed and energy of a man twenty years younger and his brain only rests when he has finished a thirteen-hour day and is asleep in his bed. It is this remarkable drive and will to succeed that has taken him to the head of a major public company and made him one of the most astute businessmen in Britain. He is also David's main sponsor and friend.

Talking to him at the Harris Queensway Group's headquarters in Orpington was like trying to catch a whirlwind which had just whipped itself up and was beginning to spin into action. He acts quickly, thinks even faster and leaves lesser men wondering how on earth they are going to keep in touch. He is also a man who cares deeply about those who work for him and the horses his company owns. Success breeds success through hard work and dedication and Phil Harris knows all about that. He started with three carpet shops at the age of seventeen when his father died and now runs at least 350.

'I used to ride when I was young but nothing very serious; my father bought me a pony called Vixen and I used to mess about on that. My love of show jumping goes a long way back, and the first show jumper I ever owned was called Warlord, whom my wife Pauline qualified for Wembley. He was a Foxhunter then and after a while Jabeena Maslin started riding him, before I sent the horse to George Hobbs. Within three months he had taken him to Barcelona for his first international, jumped two clear rounds in the Nations Cup and finished second in the Grand Prix!'

Hobbs, now retired, was then one of our top riders and when Mrs Harris gave up competitive riding she and her husband bought several more horses and put them into training with him. It was a very good partnership but Harris wanted to increase his show jumping string.

He then turned to David who was, at that time, still riding for Esso and had no idea that Phil Harris was interested in buying some horses for him to ride.

'He was the best in the world but I watched him compete for a long time before finally putting my ideas to him. He didn't know me well and I had to chase him about for a week before we got together and started to discuss the future. I told him that my aim was to buy a horse for him which was capable of winning a gold medal at the Olympics and, although he listened, it was months before anything constructive happened. When we had worked out the details I went out and bought a horse called Cranham King but, instead of having a horse fit for the Olympics, he turned out to be an absolute flop.'

Having a dream shattered in such a short space of time would have destroyed many owners, but not Harris. He continued to keep searching for the right jumper and when David found Sportsman both knew that they had something special, and Harris thought that his gold medal might soon be within reach . . . .

'I decided to go on because I knew that in show jumping success does not come overnight and the only thing to do was to keep on trying and not give up. Sportsman arrived on the scene and was, indeed, later selected for the Olympics, but David thought he was too young to risk and I came round to his way of thinking. It was a big disappointment, I admit, but he was the rider and knew the horse far better than me. That's the great thing about him – he doesn't think of winning as a means to an end. His first thought is always for his horses and, no matter what the prize is, they always come first. Our next job was to get a good team of horses which would keep us at the top and when I first bought them they were all owned by me personally and not by Harris Carpets.

'After two years, David decided that it would be best for the company to take them from me because the firm was known by the public and I wasn't. It meant, of course, that the company had free advertising which turned out to be a great asset. I now find it a bit embarrassing being the chairman of a public company and having show jumping as a hobby, but my directors are fully behind me and agree that the sport is a very good way of advertising.'

Although Harris has made his way to the top in business, success has in no way changed the man and he considers it his duty to look after the people who work for him. They have all come a long way together and, if he has his way, will go even further. Hard work stimulates him and his brain works like a computer when figures are being thrown at him.

'I'll never change. I like my business going well and I love working and keeping people happy. That's what makes the world go round. I normally work a six-day week from about 9.00 a.m. until 7.00 p.m. and then go home and start again, on the telephone. One of the reasons I love show jumping is that I find it helps me to relax.'

But what does he think of the man who rides for him?

'His best qualities are kindness to horses and, as a rider, his ability to see a stride from a long way out when he's competing. He is brilliant.

'Although we have done very well, we are always looking to improve our team and I am forever getting on to David about that. He has a tendency to think we have enough but that is not the case. We need to be searching constantly for good young horses because a rider is only as good as the animals he rides.

'I always tell him that he doesn't have to worry about the older ones, because they will keep on battling away for him as long as they

can. But they cannot go on for ever and we must have others ready to take over when they retire.

'My favourite horse is Philco. I like his style of jumping and it pleases me to see him win, probably because I had almost to force David into buying him when we were in Florida. Frank Kernan and I really had to push him to get him to agree. He wasn't worried about the horse's ability but the amount of money that was being asked for him. That's another good thing about him: he always worries about the money I spend. Not many people know this but, when the deal for Philco was done, David didn't sleep for two nights because he was

Pauline Harris at Olympia pinning the rosette on Philco

Phil and Pauline Harris

concerned about how much I had paid for the horse. You see, with him it's a business *and* a friendship.'

Harris is also a man who likes to back his rider to the hilt and, whenever David is riding abroad, he tries his hardest to fly out with him and give him support. To date he has visited some twelve countries, including South Africa, America, Germany and Holland. He considers that the best moment of his show jumping career came when the team David led won the 1978 World Championships in Aachen.

'That was the biggest thrill of all and I loved every minute of that competition. But I will never forget what he did in 1975 at Wembley's Horse of the Year show on Sportsman, Philco and Heatwave when he won seven out of eleven competitions and was second in two others. I told Pauline that, if he made it eight, I would buy her a mink coat, and you can imagine how she felt when David just didn't make it. I saved a lot of money, but I am sure she thinks he did it on purpose.'

That is a long-standing joke between them but both Phil Harris and his wife still take regular holidays with David and his wife Elizabeth. The last one they had was in South Africa, where David had accepted an invitation to ride. Harris remembers it well.

'It made a change because we both get a bit bored with holidays after a week and so this, we

64

Harris Home Care (above) *reaching for a clear round at Arena North . . .*

. . . and Sportsman (right) *over the gate*

Opposite above left: *Queensway's Special on home ground at the Wales and West*

Opposite above right: *Mister Softee heading for the European title at Hickstead in 1969*

Opposite below: *Philco showing how it should be done at the Benson & Hedges Championships in the grounds of Cardiff Castle*

thought, would be an ideal way of having a rest and at the same time do a bit of show jumping. But things started to go wrong from the start.'

Pauline Harris continued the story.

'We were based in Cape Town, and one evening we decided to get into the car and drive out to the coast for a couple of hours and watch the sea. But, instead of parking the hire car when we arrived, we drove it right on to the beach and got as near to the water's edge as we could. The only thing was it began to sink in the soft sand and we got well and truly stuck. We tried for ages to move it, but couldn't and poor David became angrier and angrier.

'But, when we had almost given up hope and visualized the car being covered by sea water, six large coloured fellows appeared from nowhere, lifted the car up and put it back on firm sand again. It really was incredible.'

Although both David and Harris work hard, they each have a great sense of humour and are forever playing jokes on one another. In the West Indies though, while they were on holiday, one of the jokes backfired and very nearly ended in disaster. For some reason or other, Harris was pushed into the hotel swimming pool and nobody thought much of it until he failed to surface. It was then David realized he couldn't swim.

'It seems,' said Harris, 'that water plays a great part in our lives. I remember another incident when we were in Sweden together sharing a hotel room. David is the sort of person who never worries even if he knows he is due to ride in a class. He doesn't make a move until he has to. Well, the particular competition we had entered on this occasion was a Gamblers Stakes, which was due to start at nine o'clock in the morning. At 8.30 we were still in our beds and David wouldn't budge.

'I gave him another couple of minutes and kept on calling for him to get up but he wouldn't; so I went into the bathroom, filled a bowl full of water and threw it over him. That got him up but the next thing I knew was that another lot of water was being poured over me so it went on until the whole room was awash.

'We arrived at the show as the second competitor was leaving the arena and David had to dash to the stables, saddle his horse and get back as fast as he could. Once he had told me to study the course, he left to make the horse ready. He returned about ten minutes later and asked me the best line to take. Well, I had been so busy drying myself off that I had only watched one horse jump and hadn't got a clue. Anyway, I told him what I thought was best and then left him to it. I think he finished sixth.

'That's part of the fun of going away with him because, no matter what happens, he takes it all in good part and nothing, but nothing, upsets him. That South African trip was also funny because, apart from the incident with the car, it was a time I did manage to get him out of bed. We had had a good, late night and David decided it was time he went to bed and left the party to go to his room. The moment he had gone I contacted one of the hotel waiters and told him that Mr Broome wanted his breakfast sent up to him at six o'clock. It was complete fabrication, of course.

'The following morning, a woman duly appeared with a trayful of food and knocked on his door. David, half asleep and standing with a towel round his waist opened it, the towel fell down around his ankles and the tray of food went crashing to the floor.

'The reason we often have fun and games is because we both know that it helps to break the tension and we like having a good time anyway.'

Harris recalls with less enthusiasm the time David – thinking that riders from all other major equestrian nations would follow Britain's lead – turned professional.

'He lost his chance of ever winning a gold medal then and he really thought that his rivals from abroad would be asked to do the same. But it didn't turn out that way and I think he was upset about it because I have always firmly believed that he wanted to win a gold.'

Harris and his wife Pauline have four children: Susan, who like her parents loves riding, Martin, and Charles and Peter who are twins. All have been sent to very good schools and are delightful youngsters.

Everyone likes to watch a champion – David with Queensway's Big Q

In the garden of his home, Harris has a large swimming pool with sauna baths tucked away at the bottom of the lawn. He is a man who enjoys the good things of life and it is right that he should be able to, because he has made his way to the top in business the hard way. And, although he is used to giving orders at his place of work, he doesn't ever impose his wishes upon his rider.

'I always leave the horses' programmes to David, because he knows exactly where and when they should compete. It wouldn't be fair of me to tell him what to do because he knows the sport better than me. But we always keep in touch and will phone each other two or three times a week even if he is riding abroad. But I always know when things aren't going too well, when he is competing overseas, because he doesn't ring.'

Apart from his sponsorship of David, Harris also takes a keen interest in putting up prize money for shows, as well. He has ploughed cash into classes at Olympia, has had his own full show at Towerlands and is the main sponsor at the Broomes' own show in Wales.

This season, when his business commitments allow, he will be seen at most of the major meetings, watching and waiting and wondering just when he will see another horse to add to his team. And when he buys an expensive one, David is certain to have a few more sleepless nights.

7 The International Riders Club

As well as being one of the best show jumping riders in the world, David is also president of the International Riders Club, an organization which was created to look after the interests of those who ride horses. He has very strong opinions on matters concerning his colleagues and explains why the club was created.

'About four years ago, the International Equestrian Federation had a major discussion on the pain-killer butazolidin and, if you feel that someone is interfering with your career, or future, you get annoyed and should do something about it. We thought – the riders, that is – that the only way to do it was as a body because basically riders are a rabble. They never pull together and always want to do their own thing. Anyway, the club was formed. I don't know how much power we have to our elbow but whenever we meet the FEI (Federation Equestre Internationale) now it is as a body and not as individuals. For the first couple of years we were lucky to have Raimondo d'Inzeo as our president and I think he did a good job. But one of the rules of the International Riders Club is that you have to be an active member and, just over a year ago, in Amsterdam, I was elected president. I don't know how long it will be for – I suppose that is up to the members – but I have, in my term of office, met Prince Philip on behalf of the club.

'I must admit, though, that the driving force behind me is my number two, Paul Schockemohle. He is a dynamic character who knows and feels that the club is a good thing for all concerned. Without him I am sure we wouldn't have done as well as we have. He certainly makes me think deeply about things and that can't be bad. The trouble with many of our members is that they think that, if things

are good enough for Paul and me, they are good enough for them, and they don't get involved too much. Despite this, I think that the club is a good thing and that we are now recognized, which is important.'

In Paris in 1978, the question of butazolidin was discussed at length by the FEI, as it had been the year before and, by the time you read this book, everyone will know if 'bute' has been banned for competition horses in this country. It is an emotive subject, which many riders feel strongly about, and one to which David has given a lot of thought with the welfare of his horses uppermost in his mind.

'One of their attitudes was that a lot of riding schools throughout the world were giving it to their horses for breakfast in order to keep them sound. My answer to that is that whatever has been decided about the use of 'bute' in show jumping is not going to alter what people may do in some riding schools. So, in my opinion, they shouldn't concern themselves with it. As far as the sport is concerned, it needs its stars and some of those horses who have reached that position have had some wear and tear over the years. So why should they not be given the benefit of modern medication? The proposition we put forward was that we thought horses should be able to have bute as long as it was given under the supervision of a show's vet. I think one of the things the FEI was worried about was the public response to "drugs". What we are talking about is medication.'

Some people fear that there are riders who might abuse the situation and use bute on their horses when and as often as they felt like it.

'Yes, I understand that but, if you go to a show and hand in your horse's passport, it could be recorded in there what a horse should

David Broome with Paul Schockemohle, number two in the International Riders Club and a dynamic character

be given. And that document would have to be signed by a vet. What's wrong with that?'

Will a lot of show jumpers be able to compete without bute, or will they simply fade away from the scene?

'Lots of the older ones will drop out and that will include some of the stars, too. I think bute should be allowed, provided it is administered under veterinary supervision.'

Now that the International Riders Club has been formed and is recognized, do you believe that its members would ever boycott a show?

'Not as a body, no, I don't think it would. And the only way it could happen is if every one of the members decided that he or she didn't want to ride. On that theme, and as the club's president, I know I would never call a strike. I haven't the power to do that and I think it is right that I shouldn't be able to do so.'

The International Riders Club does send delegates to F E I meetings but does not have a vote, and that is a situation David would like to see changed as soon as possible.

'The F E I has become an enormous body: it

After each round of the World Cup competition in 1979,
a representative of the Dutch Ministry of Agriculture
presented the winner with a silver tulip

represents something like 126 nations and each one has an equal vote; even though Britain and West Germany probably contribute more financially than anyone else, they still have the same vote as a minor nation – even over an important question like bute. It's crackers. There is so much dissent around from national federations that, if the FEI is not very careful, they might find themselves running their own world thing while we have our European crowd. It could happen.

'At one stage we had about 130 members of the International Riders Club and each member had to pay a subscription fee of £25. But it became such a hassle collecting the money from different people that what we are trying to do now is take half a per cent of a rider's prize money at international shows and get the organizers of those shows to send it direct to us. If anyone objects to that system however, they can have their money back. What we are trying to do is speed things up and at the same time plan things so that everyone benefits from any moves we make.

'The club was started when the bute debate came up. I was in Dortmund at the time and told Paul Schockemohle that I thought we should have a meeting about it with Max Ammann, who was a Swiss newspaper editor. He was the shining light behind us all and set it up very well. He is a man with a very strong character and that held us all together and got things moving. He has left us now, but we are going to kick on because we have recently appointed my agent, Lister Welch, as the club's managing director. And I feel that we should go ahead and be a small nucleus, strong but without any grand ideas. We just want our interests to be looked after.'

One competition all the riders like is the World Cup which, in its first year of operation, had its final in Gothenburg; and last season it was held in Baltimore.

'Overall I think it has been good for everyone, including the press.'

But did it not prevent some young riders from being sent abroad because senior members of British show jumping always wanted to ride in the European qualifiers, thereby cutting down the number of places available for youngsters?

'That is a good question and, basically, I suppose that is true. But, let's face it, the idea of the World Cup was to try and bind together the winter shows, to give them a league and make it more interesting. And until the World Cup was formed these young riders you are talking about didn't want to go abroad in the winter.

'It's only now that there is a great big carrot available that they want to go abroad and are screaming their heads off because they think we are being selfish. But let's get it straight. We have been going abroad to some of those shows for more than twenty years and, now something useful has been created, they want to get in on the act. I'm sorry, but it's a hard life and I'm afraid I don't have much sympathy for them. Having made that clear, it is true to say that everyone does have a chance to go in the World Cup.'

Although some of the youngsters may think that they are being hard done by, the World Cup has caused an enormous amount of interest, although several members of the public did express the view that they found the final in Baltimore last year hard to follow. It may well be so at present, but with experts running the competition things can only get better. It must also be mentioned that last year the Dutch put up a lot of money towards the staging of the qualifying contests, as did Volvo; and after each round representatives from Holland presented the winner with a silver tulip worth £200. With that financial support and the hard-working organizers, the World Cup has been a great success and proves beyond doubt that show jumping is growing rapidly not only in Britain but in other countries as well.

8 How It All Started

David began riding at the age of two and a half and by the time he was five had graduated to breaking Welsh ponies for his father. They were years he thoroughly enjoyed until one day he took one fall too many during a pony-schooling session and decided to call it a day.

'It just happened that I was thrown once too often and gave up riding for a total of eighteen months. In fact, I wouldn't go near a horse and I think this was when my father played things very cleverly. He knew what I was going through and didn't force me to ride. When I had reached the grand old age of six and a half, I suddenly wanted to start helping him with the ponies.

'The moment I told him I was interested again he gave me so much help and encouragement it made it all worth while, and I remember him going out and buying me a pony called Coffee. He could really jump and one day my father asked me if I would like to go hunting with him. Well, we set off, went across a couple of fields to a covert and the hounds found. When it was over, he told me that I had to go the long way back because there was a large post and rails to negotiate and he thought it would be safer for me to give it a miss.

'I wasn't going to have any of that and told my father that, if he was going to jump it, so was I and, instead of telling me I couldn't, he agreed and off we went. It was a great feeling jumping that fence and since the pony was a bit useful it all became a challenge and I started to take him show jumping.'

But the young man who, much later, was to become champion of the world was to find that taking part in competition was vastly different to jumping a post and rails while out hunting. He was also to have his first taste of publicity.

'The first show I ever went to didn't end that well for me because the class I was riding in had a 3 foot 9 inch wall and, as we jumped it, I went back into the saddle as the pony's back end was coming up. The next thing I knew I was sitting on the grass wondering what had happened. The next day the local paper carried a picture of me which simply said underneath, 'D. Broome – falling off'.

That initial mishap, however, only fired his enthusiasm and it wasn't long before he was going to as many shows as his schooling would allow.

'That was when things became somewhat difficult because my mother was always keen that we should have a good education and at that time I was even going to school on Saturday, the one day when most of the shows were taking place. And even if there was one on in mid-week I wasn't allowed to go because schooling had to come first.

'But, by the time I was fifteen, we used to have a couple of hours we could use as private study and this was where my education really came in useful. I would make sure that my two hours off came towards the end of the morning and, when everyone thought I was in the library swotting, I would be off out of it and making my way to one of the local shows. I did that for a year without anyone catching on.'

During that time he was also asked by the school's careers officer what he wanted to do when his studies were over. David wanted to be a genius with horses and ponies, like his father, and he wanted to stay with his father as long as he possibly could.

'But those who were doing the asking would never have understood, so when they kept on I just replied that I intended to be a vet.

A young David Broome at home

'That seemed to please everyone, but the truth was I had my heart set on being a show jumper and learning as much from my father as I possibly could. He was always the brains where horses were concerned and without him I wouldn't have had a chance. He would study their feeding, shoeing and every little detail to make sure they were getting everything they needed. If we ever went to a show and had a bad day, it was always father who had the sleepless nights trying to work out what went wrong. When we took three ponies to a show and I didn't jump nine clear rounds, he wasn't satisfied. Without that total dedication to what we were doing I would never be where I am today.'

Two other people of whom he speaks in glowing terms are Colonel Sir Harry Llewellyn and Pat Smythe, who were among the great show jumping riders of all time.

'They lived nearby and helped me a lot during my career. They were stars and I admired them greatly, particularly Pat. You only had to listen to my father on the way back from a show to know how good she was and, because of that, I used to study the way she rode. Sir Harry was and still is a great source of encouragement, and I have a great respect for him.'

David first rode in adult classes at the Carmarthen show when he was sixteen, on two horses called Golden Noble and Spot of Gold. He didn't win and was, in fact, eliminated in one of the events on Spot of Gold. But he will always remember the man who did triumph.

'That was Warwick Woodhall, and his prize was £50. When he was unsaddling the horse I went round to his stable and all I kept thinking about was the money. It seemed such an awful lot for winning a show jumping class.'

In 1957 David's father saw a young horse he thought had a lot of potential and went out and bought him for the princely sum of £60. It was one of the best moves he made.

'Wildfire was a horse different from anything else I had ever sat on; he was like a bouncing ball. You just had to ask him to do something and he did it. He had all the ability in the world, even though he appeared to the onlooker to be nasty tempered and generally sour. He wasn't either of those things and I loved him. The second year I had him he went out and won a total of £1000 and the season after that he was the leading money winner. He was, without any shadow of a doubt, my first star.'

Show jumping is now one of the major growth sports, but the thousands of people who go to shows or watch them on television often do not realize the amount of hard work that goes on behind the scenes. There is also a lot of

Colonel Sir Harry Llewellyn on his famous horse Foxhunter in 1953

pain suffered, and even now David wears a corset to combat an old injury.

'It happened in 1968 when I was riding in Toronto and had a fall on Mister Softee. I got back on again okay but, when I went to kick

David Broome in 1962 on Wildfire, the horse who was 'without a shadow of a doubt, my first star'

Four of the riders in training to represent Britain in the 1960 Olympic Games in Rome. Left to right: Anne Townsend on Bandit, David Barker on Franco, Pat Smythe on Flanagan and David Broome on Wildfire

him on, I couldn't move and had to be helped from the saddle. Within minutes, the organizers of the show had taken me to a

75

Show jumping wasn't always a solemn business

doctor, a huge Irishman, who diagnosed muscle trouble and proceeded to give me an almighty thump on the back. I don't know if it was that or the fall, but the plain truth is that I have never been the same since. Now I find that the best thing for me to do is wear a corset – not for support but to keep the back muscles warm. On several occasions the injury has really given me a lot of pain and when it becomes severe I just have to rest until I am perfectly fit again.'

The muscle trouble also means that he has to be extremely careful about what he does, and he knows that he made a dreadful mistake when competing at the Dublin show in 1977.

'Apart from some first-class jumping competitions, they also had Pony Club games and someone had the bright idea that it would be great fun for the British show jumping team to take part. Harvey Smith, who was with me at the time, knew all about the pain I had suffered with my back, and he told me that I was mad even to think of going in the wheelbarrow race that had been devised.

'Anyway, instead of listening to his advice, off I went and started pushing this damn wheelbarrow across the ring, with one of the other riders sitting inside. Halfway across the handle broke and instead of pulling out I carried on and grabbed the side of the thing. Well, we raced across the finishing line and suddenly my back went again.

'For twenty-four hours I was a cripple and was doubled up in pain. The journey home was absolute murder and, when I did finally make it, I had to spend the next eighteen days lying on my lounge carpet. That was the only way I could get any relief from the dreadful pain. In the end, Mr Lewis, who looks after the Welsh Rugby team put me right and after seeing him I was riding again within three weeks. But, do you know, when your back goes, it feels like the end of the world.'

Having a damaged back is one of the worst injuries a show jumping rider can have because the muscles and the spine have to be in constant use. Alwin Shockemohle, the former West German show jumping star and winner of an individual gold medal in Montreal, gave up show jumping because of his back injury.

Apart from damaged muscles, David has also broken his right leg – an accident he will never forget because at the time he didn't think the fall was bad enough to hurt him.

'That happened at Wembley when a mare I was riding fell on her knees and toppled over sideways. I thought at the time that all I had to do was roll away from her and everything would be fine. But it didn't quite happen like that. As she keeled over, I fell on one of the show jumping poles and wrapped my right leg around it. There was a very loud crack and the bone snapped. I must say, that really did hurt.'

The injuries do not really worry him because he knows that he must soldier on regardless. What does upset him, however, are some of the stories the media carries about him.

'Very rarely do we get as much credit as those in other sports; but, whenever anything goes wrong, we hit the headlines. It's the same for Harvey: if he makes a mistake, the next moment it's either in the papers or on television. But I suppose that is part of the penalty to pay for being show jumpers.'

Hit the headlines David did in 1973, when the British Show Jumping Association announced that he had become a professional. Many of those who follow the sport were shocked at the decision because it meant that he would never be allowed to ride in the Olympic Games – unless the rules were changed.

'To be perfectly honest, that was on the cards a long time before it actually happened. Harvey and I had talked it over lots of times and had decided that we would eventually turn professional. I remember when the form came from the show jumping authorities instructing me to fill it in, asking if I wanted an amateur licence or professional permit. I just enclosed £1 and sent it back unsigned, just to see what would happen. About a fortnight later it was returned with a professional rider's licence inside with the registration number 003. But I never did actually sign anything. Their reasoning was that because I rode for several owners I must be professional. They would never get away with that on those grounds today.'

But what was his reaction to not being able to take part in future Olympics?

'I suppose I was a bit disappointed at the time, but the last Games I had ridden in, at Munich in 1972 on Manhattan, hadn't gone very well. And, as they are only staged every four years anyway, I just accepted the fact that my chance of winning a gold medal was remote. I also had the opportunity to make some money as a professional rider.'

Keeping horses is an expensive pastime but for a show jumper the expenses are frightening, and without sponsorship many would not be able to carry on competing.

'Up to two years ago, the costs of keeping my team of show jumpers on the circuit came to £50,000 annually. And that is without buying new horses and marking down the old ones. I have to earn at least that amount of money to break even, which means a lot of hard work.'

Apart from his show jumping activities,

David Broome comes to grief on Ballywillwill at Hickstead, 1969

David has also broadened his horizons and gone into the carpet business with his brother Frederick. He, too, used to ride and had many fine successes to his credit.

'Frederick was somewhat unfortunate when he was riding because he was forever living under my shadow and that could not have been easy for him. Plus the fact that, at the time he was in show jumping, I was riding all the good horses anyway so that it was really an uphill battle.

'But he is keen on the carpet business and eventually we decided to set up with a couple of shops of our own. He's very good at the business side of things and I think everything will turn out well.'

9 Mount Ballan Manor

Finding the Broome family home is about as difficult as discovering the whereabouts of Buckingham Palace. Visitors from the South of England drive across the Severn Bridge, stop and ask the nearest Welshman for directions. That is the measure of the Broomes' popularity.

'I suppose altogether we farm about 350 acres, a little of which is arable but it's mainly grassland for sheep and cattle. My parents have lived at Mount Ballan Manor for some thirty years and I expect I will be there for another thirty. I love the place and have no desire to go

At home in the stable yard with Queensway's Big Q and Queensway's Special

anywhere else. In the yard we have about twenty-five stables and, when we put on the Wales and West Shows, we can increase that number by 250 with the wooden ones made from the timber which my father hauled home with his own hands; they are just right for accommodating the horses which attend our shows and the interesting thing is that they were all made from second-hand wood.

'We hold three main shows a year and are very lucky to have Harris Carpets and Monsanto as sponsors, as well as Everest Double Glazing and Radio Rentals, but I must say a special word of thanks to the smaller sponsors who put up the prizes for all the minor

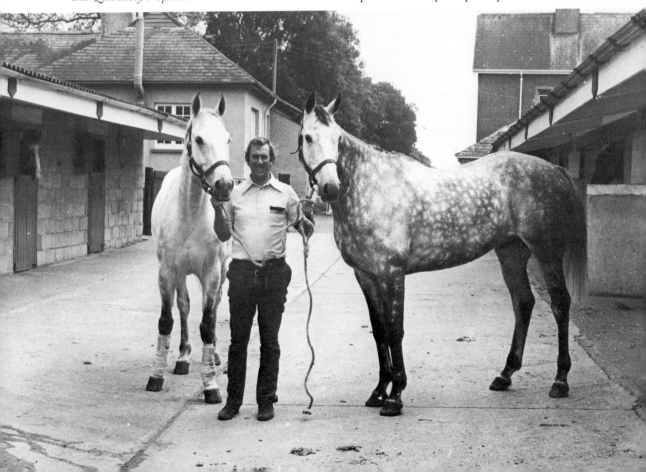

A young David with Tubby

Philco's first workout of the season

classes. They are as important as the others. It was my father who decided that we would turn part of the farm into a showground because it had always been a dream of his, and I consider myself very fortunate in having been able to help make that dream a reality, even though he doesn't make a penny from the shows.

'We started running them about nine years ago and anyone who thinks the courses are built to suit me has only to look at the record books. When we first started we had a habit of digging a new ditch on the course before every meeting so that the riders would always come along and find something different. When I think about it, I have been eliminated at that ditch more than anyone else, so it certainly wasn't put there with me in mind and, out of the seven Welsh Derbys we have put on, I have won only

one. Out of a hundred classes in the main ring I have taken only four, so I think anyone can see that there certainly isn't any favouritism.

'Apart from staging activities for the seniors, we also try and make sure that juniors get a look in as well. After all, that is how we all started. Those events have proved very popular with the public and make good supporting programmes. My father is very keen on driving and has four Welsh Cob stallions but, when we staged a full driving show at Mount Ballan Manor, it didn't get the support we had hoped for and I don't think we will be doing it again.'

Although David has been deeply involved in show jumping for the past twenty-five years, his first love now is farming and you can almost feel the pleasure he gets from it when he is talking about the estate.

'It helps keep me sane because when I leave the shows I can come back home, jump on a tractor and leave the other world behind. It helps me to relax because I know that I don't have to watch the clock and can just settle down and get stuck into the job in hand. It's not brainy work I do and, as my man on the farm, Cliff Williams, says, "You can't educate pork" – that is the term he uses to describe me. But I really do love it all.

'Cliff has been with us for twenty years and is like a brother to me. But I must be honest. I am not a six-o'clock-in-the-morning farmer. I do, on the other hand, work late into the night and am often on the telephone at ten or even eleven at night, so it's as broad as it is long.'

There is one aspect of farming that makes David angry and causes him to start talking about the facts and figures of land. Profit is a word big businessmen use in the City with gay abandon. But not him.

David driving at the Wales and West Show with Chief Inspector Dick Cheetham

'Not making any money out of it all really upsets me, because everyone on the farm works very hard and I am not just saying that to gain any sympathy. Just assume that you pay £2500 an acre for land. If you were to invest that money for a year at an interest rate of 10 per cent there would be a return of £250 on your capital. But, when you buy land for that same amount, the best you can hope for is something like £50. That is the one thing about farming that I do not like and never will. Farming isn't a way of making money; it is purely and simply a way of life and it is one with which you have to come to terms. Having said that, however, I do think we are privileged to be able to go out and walk about the estate and think, "That's mine." It is a tremendous feeling because you are not beholden to anyone. My parents have earned the right to do that because they have worked hard all their lives and deserve what they have got.

'When Liz and I were first married we

The Broome family at the Wales and West Show. Left to right: *Mrs Broome, Fred, David, Ballan Lad, Mary, Liz Edgar and Fred senior*

moved into one of the semi-detached bungalows, but now we have built another house on the farm which my parents will move into and Liz, James and me will live in their house. When father bought the farm, he also purchased the mansion next door and the family home is actually the old stage coach and grooms' stables which were converted. It has all taken time to get right but it is a great place to live and I will be there for the rest of my days.'

The first question any woman would ask is how does David's wife Elizabeth get on living so close to her in-laws?

'I think in any family in-laws are a problem – it is only human nature. But both sides of my family are very good because they try very hard and we all understand the problems which can arise. Understanding is halfway to winning and that is why we all get on very well and it works.'

There is no doubt that he had a very contented childhood and has fond memories of Mount Ballan Manor, the farm and school.

'I used to have lots of fun as a kid but the thing that really sticks out in my mind are the early days at school. I was at Monmouth Grammar for about six years and we would be set certain projects to do about the surrounding area. And I will always remember the time we all went to Raglan Castle and I set to work writing an epic on what I had seen, and illustrated it with drawings of the castle. I was so proud of it and went all out to win the prize. In all, I think it came to about thirteen pages, but all I won was a commendation – not for merit, but for effort. I suppose the sheer bulk of the stuff impressed them. A few years later we did the same project, but instead of going again I went shooting squirrels with a friend and just rewrote the first page of the original text.'

The Broomes employ several stable staff to

look after the horses and ponies at Mount Ballan Manor and everyone lives as one big happy family, even though they all know the amount of work involved.

'We usually have about five girls looking after things and I am lucky because, when we

Opposite above: *Preparing for a trip abroad*

Opposite below: '*Jumping on a tractor and leaving the world of the shows behind keeps me sane*'

David being greeted affectionately by Herman the German, otherwise known as Queensway's Big Q

take on any new girls, Mary takes them under her wing and educates them in our ways.

'In fact, Tina, who had been with us for six years, left last year. To be fair to young girls, there is more to life than looking after other people's horses. And Tina really did love them. But, at the end of the day, you can understand why they move on because I suppose they think they are getting into a rut. It was a thing Tina and I never spoke about, but I did stop her leaving once before with a bit of charm and persuasion. On the last occasion, however, I didn't feel I would be right trying to keep her there. When she first arrived six years ago, I didn't think she would last more that a couple of days because she was, then, very timid. But she was good and certainly proved me wrong.'

Do the girls ever have the chance of taking part in competitions when they work for him?

'On the odd occasion, if they are capable, I might let that happen but not on any of my Grand Prix horses, because that just wouldn't be feasible. But they do ride the horses every day at exercise.'

Having horses around the stables means that there must be transport available at all times to take them to the many shows they attend throughout the year. David has three horseboxes.

'That is where a lot of expense comes in because they only do about twelve or fourteen miles to the gallon and, when you are doing a long journey, the costs soon begin to add up. They are also very expensive to buy and the big one I have would cost something like £35,000. Now it is easy to see why I have to make at least £50,000 a year to break even.'

10 The British Show Jumping Association

Kenilworth, in Warwickshire, is not only a small, lovely part of the English countryside; it is also a place where the British Show Jumping Association has its headquarters. It is somewhat like walking into an army camp where everything is kept clean and tidy and even the buildings, of which there are many, seem to stand to attention as if they know their place. The BSJA has direct control of show jumping and has done a good job steering it in the right direction. Any rider participating in the sport has to be a member and, rightly, abide by its rules.

'I first joined it some twenty or more years ago and became a life member for about £25. Now, however, it would cost a lot more for life membership. I am also a selector – a role I enjoy very much because, apart from choosing those who are to go on teams, I help to send them abroad to go and do a job and, if they do it well, it's a good feeling. In the last five years or more I have been very lucky because I have seen most of the horses and riders compete and know exactly what they can do. With that experience, I think I am qualified to talk about selection along with three or four of my colleagues and I don't think we have done a bad job when you look at the records.'

There are, though, some people who would say that a rider should not be on any selection committee because he might have a tendency to pick himself.

'Well, there might be a certain amount of truth in that but, when I reach the stage when I can't stand up and argue that I made the right decision, then that will be the day I get chucked off or will want to resign.

'Any decision I have ever made has been done honestly and above board. Those who choose the teams base their choice on merit and try to avoid favouritism. It is a very honourable committee which does the job and I am proud to be part of it. We have made one or two ticklish decisions, particularly where Harvey Smith and his son Robert are concerned but, on reflection, I wouldn't alter one of them because we have always picked the best teams in the fairest way possible.'

Has he ever been accused of putting himself first?

'No, I don't think I have, and – to bring a point home – last year I went to the Devon County Show, won two good classes and four days later was chucked off the team for Hickstead because Philco was unwell. The results at Devon, it seems, didn't count, but I still happen to think that they chose a very good team for the Nations Cup. So you may talk about injustices but there was certainly no favouritism there. If people level accusations at me, they have just got to look back and they will see that I can be dropped just the same as anyone else and that is the way it should be. It seems that people never see their own case as fairly as they should do. What is difficult about the job is telling some doting father that his daughter is not as good as he thought she was. I must say it's not very pleasant to have to say that and sometimes those concerned do get a bit frustrated, because they think their sons and daughters are being held back. You can't blame a parent for that; in fact you try to sympathize with them, but you still have a duty to pick the best team possible from those who want to go and I always feel that we do just that. There are about eleven or twelve

Colonel Sir Harry Llewellyn with Colonel Sir Michael Ansell, pictured together at Hickstead, 1975

members of the selection committee and the BSJA does the best with the resources it has; it's always easy to say it could be improved.'

That is, of course, very true, but as a rider is he happy with the way the sport in which he makes a living is being run?

'I think the BSJA should make more money from the shows it runs because, in my view, they get a pittance out of it. If you run a £350,000 operation, put the sponsors in, organize TV and finish up with £14,000, I think it is a joke. Those people should be entitled to, say, 10 per cent of it all. Anyone who puts up the prize money is, I would have thought, entitled to that. The British Show

Jumping Association is hard up and will continue to be so unless it re-thinks its policies.'

Apart from that, does he think that the BSJA has made a valuable contribution to show jumping.

'There is no doubt about that whatsoever, because the sport has continued to grow over the past twenty years. It's all very well for the knockers to criticize but, if you think what prize money we used to jump for in the old days and what we do now, it is easy to see that everyone has benefited.'

There might be those who thought the BSJA made a blunder over the issue of calling horses by trade names a few years ago, when they said one thing and eventually ended up doing another.

'I think it was going along nicely, but then it

went haywire because horses' names were being completely changed and the public was becoming confused. The whole thing got mucky because every Tom, Dick and Harry was jumping on the bandwagon and a halt had to be called. But we did sort it all out eventually. The name changing had to be stopped almost overnight because there were children with small ponies getting in on the act.

'When you get down to it you will find that our sport is supported by those who live in villages all over the country, who like to see how their favourite horses are going. They are the grass roots of show jumping. Now, for argument's sake, say their favourite horse was Sportsman and I changed it suddenly to Harris Quicksale, they are going to lose interest because they don't know what is going on. Something had to be done.'

Whenever anybody talks about the BSJA a man who always springs to mind is Colonel Sir Michael Ansell, an incredible person who, although blind, was responsible for putting show jumping on the map. He is now living in the West Country. What he did for the sport will probably never be equalled, or appreciated.

'He always knew exactly where we were going and, if you look at show jumping from when it started and how he left it, you can see what he did for all of us. He's a man's man and stood head and shoulders above everyone else and there will never be another like him. He is a good person who always commands respect. When we used to go abroad to ride in the early fifties and sixties he would always send us a telegram before we went in the Nations Cup which said, "Good Luck – and make sure you bloody well win." He very often telephones me now at home and asks me what I think of certain aspects of show jumping. I value his counsel because he is a man who always knows what he is doing.

'Another person I like a lot is John Blakeway, chairman of the BSJA. He is very straight and, although we have had a few rows, I have a lot of time for him because he, too, has done a lot for the sport.'

One of the biggest decisions the equestrian authorities had to make was whether to send any teams to the Moscow Olympics in 1980 after the Russians had moved into Afghanistan. Many of Britain's athletes made the trip to Moscow and competed but the equestrian competitors withdrew en masse.

'I was involved in part of that decision and I had a gut feeling it was wrong to support the Russians because there comes a time when you must stand up to the bully. If they are allowed to get away with what they are doing, it's not long before they keep taking a bit more and a bit more and somewhere along the line you have got to do something, no matter how pathetic it seems. For me there was never any question of going. I think that history is repeating itself. I also believe that because we rely on the Americans so much we should rally round our mates and not kick them in the teeth.'

Going to Moscow might have given our young amateur riders the chance of winning gold medals. Some people might have thought they had been robbed of that opportunity.

'I don't think it was such a big chance and, anyway, most of the riders we were going to send out there will be around for the next Olympics anyway. They will have their chances again.'

Some of the experts think that there should not be team competitions in the Olympic Games because they are getting too big.

'I have been to four and they are, it is true, getting enormous. I think the Games should be for individuals only and that all team events should be cut out.'

But many members of the BSJA consider that a team win is far better than individual honours.

'Probably because they have a better chance of winning a team gold than an individual one. That would be my answer to that. I would also say that it's easier to win the team contest because the individual competition is a bit of a one-off thing on the day and that, in fact, is what the Olympics are all about – the best man or woman on the day.'

11 The Day Philco Nearly Died

It was like any other day to David: there was work to do on the farm, horses to school and a thousand other jobs to complete. Everything had gone well that morning and he was looking forward to a peaceful evening at home with Liz. That night, however, Philco was to fall desperately ill and turn his world into a nightmare.

'I didn't know about it until about 9.30 that night when Mary came running up to the house and told me that he was very unwell and coughing badly. That came as a shock because we always have a look round the stables before leaving the horses at night and he was perfectly okay then.

'I knew he had some sort of allergy but it must have been dust or something in the hay which triggered it off. It really is impossible to say but, by God, was he coughing and in a state.

'So the first thing we did was to take him out of the stable and into one of the fields so that he could get some fresh air. Then we called the

Philco at the 1978 World Championships in Aachen

vet, who arrived about twenty minutes later. By this time poor Philco's gums and tongue had turned blue. After giving him a thorough examination, which included checking his heart and lungs, the vet gave him an injection which seemed to calm him a bit. When he was satisfied that everything was all right, the vet left but returned a couple of hours later to see how Philco was progressing. We were very lucky that it was such a fine night because in the end Mary and Tina stayed up all night with the horse.

'The thing was we couldn't put him back into his box because whatever had started off the coughing might do the same again unless we cleaned out the stable and gave it a good disinfecting. Actually, the vet described it as some sort of allergy, but the stuff that can be given to Philco by injection is on the list of banned substances which the FEI produces. So now we have to be very careful with him.

'Anyway, we made a very thorough job of cleaning out his stable and then, instead of putting straw down, we forked in about six bales of peat for him to stand on and at £5 a bale you can imagine how expensive it was. But then it was Philco and, frankly, money just didn't come into it.

'At the time he was coughing I didn't really know how serious it all was until I told my vet that Hickstead was coming up and did he think Philco would be all right for that because we were likely to be picked for the team. The vet informed me that there would be no chance and explained how close Philco had been to death. That shook me to the core. Apparently, when his tongue and gums had turned blue it was his blood going wrong and the actual blood count was way off the mark. He also had slightly damaged lungs and only rest and proper care was going to put him right.

'Just to make sure I fully understood the position, the vet added that, if I took him to Hickstead, I most certainly would never win and there was a chance I might even kill him. After that, Hickstead was wiped out of my mind and the main thing was getting him well again. When I phoned Phil Harris he said,

"Oh, my God, what else can go wrong? Keep me informed of his progress" – which of course, we did.

'What with Philco being very ill and poor old Manhattan dropping dead, I began to panic and think I wouldn't have any more horses left. I just couldn't work out what was going wrong. Without horses my whole life would be meaningless, because for me there is nothing else. I don't want to appear callous or offend anyone in any way, but "Hattie" was at the end of his career and had had a very good life. However, I always like to keep one really good horse available throughout the season and suddenly, at that moment, there wasn't one.

'Harris Home Care is quite good and Tabac Original's excellent – but the others are just that much better again and with the Grands Prix coming up you have to have a super class horse to win them.

'After Hattie dropped dead I had many, many letters from the public: it was a mixed bag. There were a lot of sympathetic ones but I had one or two that were really poison jobs which said that I was cruel to have been jumping him. One old lady even reported me to the RSPCA. I just feel sorry for those people because they don't appear to understand at all. Manhattan never had a bad life in any way and, even though he was eighteen when he died, it must be remembered that horses jump until they are twenty-one or even twenty-two years old. He had been competing in small classes for the last three years of his life and was terribly well. In fact, one lady journalist even said that just before he died, and I know that horsey people would agree that, if he had to go because his time was up, that was the best way for it to happen.

'I take the view that good horses are so difficult to get – much as precious stones if you like – that, when I'm lucky enough to have one, I am going to make him last as long as I can. There are so many classes to jump in these days – unlike in eventing where Badminton and Burghley and perhaps one other are the only big ones – that I can afford to pick and choose. I reckon I compete for 170 days of the year and, if

Manhattan was eighteen when he died in 1980; seen here at Hickstead in 1974

I don't think the odds are in my favour to win, I don't start. And, if the ground's bad or conditions unfair, I won't bother because there are, as I have said, many more opportunities. That policy helps me to conserve my horses and by doing that they last much longer because they haven't been overjumped. For me it is just a matter of common sense and it has paid dividends.

'After Hattie died I felt so sorry for him.

When you suffer this kind of loss it gets to you, and even though he fell and trapped my leg that was only secondary and my hurt didn't matter. Fred Welch, one of the other riders, was most kind to me: he put me in his car, drove me back to my caravan, and ten minutes later the ambulance arrived and took me to have the leg X-rayed. By this time there was an egg-size bruise on it and the spur which I had had on my boot had snapped in half under the impact of the fall.

'But the thing that sickened me about it all was the number of people who just stood there

94

looking at my horse lying on the ground. I felt then that I had let the old boy down, because I am sure animals like to go off on their own and die with dignity – not be stared at by a lot of curious people.

'Another point I didn't much like, and an incident which shows why journalism sometimes gets a bad name, was when my mother had a phone call shortly after my wife Liz had phoned and told her what had happened. Directly she put the phone down my mother said a reporter got through and just said, "Is is true that Manhattan is dead and David has broken a leg?" If Liz hadn't told her beforehand, it would have been one hell of a shock for her. I don't know how I would have handled it as a journalist but at the time it just appeared to be a bit brutal. I understand they have a job to do and know that it's not easy, but, when you and your own family are involved, you see things in a different light.

'When I had finished at the hospital, I went back to my caravan on the showground but could hardly sleep because the leg was giving me so much pain. The following morning I got up to go and have a wash and decided to try and put a fur-lined wellington boot on the injured leg, to see if it would make the going just a little bit easier. Well, as the morning progressed the leg did get a little better so I decided to go and pay a few saddler's bills and, at the same time, have a look at the course for that afternoon's Lancia class, which in fact was a qualifier for the final.

'Most of the qualifying rounds for this particular competition are staged throughout the winter, when I am usually abroad, and so you can imagine how I felt when I thought I was going to allow a golden opportunity to qualify go by. When it came round to the class, I watched a few horses jump and all the time my leg was getting better and the pain easing

off. As I had entered all my horses for the week, I went to Mrs Barnes in the collecting ring and said, with tongue in cheek, "Technically I suppose I'm not undeclared – am I?"

'As you know, earlier at the show I had had a bit of a row over declaration and didn't really know how this would be taken. But Mrs Barnes replied, "No David, I don't suppose you are – but everyone told me last night you wouldn't be going today."

'So I said, "Well, I wonder if, were I to go and get my horse, you would allow me to start?"

'The next thing was she had phoned the judges, got the okay and I drove back to my caravan and told a very startled wife and groom that I intended to compete in the class. They got Harris Home Care saddled up and I went in the ring with one ordinary boot on and the other placed firmly inside a wellington – and finished third to qualify for the final.'

That made David feel a little better but the death of such a fine, much loved horse was still stabbing at the hearts of those back at his home.

'Mary was very upset and Tina, who as you know had left us, was told by her over the phone so that she wouldn't first hear the news about Hattie on the radio or see it on television. And Wendy, one of my other grooms, also took it badly because they all loved the horse. The worst thing of all was seeing his empty stable and knowing he wouldn't be in there again.

'So what I did to ease the blow was put another horse in the box, so that it was at least occupied and the girls were not staring into an empty space and upsetting themselves. I suppose the nearest thing to it is when one of your family dies and there is an empty chair at the table and everyone looks at it and remembers. The best thing to do is take the chair away because life must go on and, if you love someone, you don't forget them anyway.'

12 Women in Show Jumping

More than two million people ride regularly in the United Kingdom and the majority of those are girls or young women. Several of them have made it to the very top in show jumping, but many fall by the wayside and cannot take the hard times, haven't the money to buy a good horse or just fail because of a lack of talent and dedication. David has seen many of those who have managed to climb the high ladder to success.

'Harvey Smith and I have been in show jumping for years and during that time we have been more bothered by girls with just one horse, than many others with two or three. Go back through our careers and you will find Marion Mould with Stroller, Alison Dawes with The Maverick, Ann Moore with Psalm, Debbie Johnsey with Moxy, Caroline Bradley with Tigre and, before those, Anneli Drummond-Hay with Merely-A-Monarch and Pat Smythe with Flanagan. There has always been a girl with a super horse and she has been a problem to beat for the years she was at the top.

'Basically it is a hard life for a girl because

Marion Mould on Elizabeth Anne II at Cardiff

Ann Moore on Psalm

they have got to get everything ready to go to a show while probably having to cope with parents who are overprotective. That's how it should be of course, but worried parents are another thing the girl has to think about. However, I do believe that there have been as many good girl riders in show jumping as men but maybe the lads stay around longer than they do. In fact, the women are marvellous and as good as us any day of the week – when they have good horses. They might even be tougher, and I know for a fact that they don't leave any stones unturned while they are in the sport.

'If ever they see an opportunity they go out and grab it with both hands and good luck to them – that is the way to go about the job. Show jumping, of course, is one of the few sports where they can compete on equal terms and the record shows they have proved to be very good at it. But, having said that, when it comes to the Olympics – the real big time – I think that men stand the pressure much better than women do. I will probably get a lot of stick for saying that but, when the chips are down and there is no messing, I think the lads can cope better than the girls. In the Olympics you will jump the biggest course you will ever jump in your life and the atmosphere in the arena is electric. You walk in and you are suddenly faced with something like 120,000 people and there is a tremendous feeling of excitement which hits you suddenly and, if you can't handle it, you freeze.

'It was like that in the 1960 Olympics in Rome and I was lucky enough to have such a good horse as Sunsalve, who took it all in his stride – but it was a terrifying feeling, and some people do crack. I tend to think it's even worse for girls and that is why Marion and Ann did so well to win their silver medals in Mexico and Munich.

'But they are both extremely good riders and Marion has jumped some very big fences at places like Hickstead on Stroller and others, and that was no fluke. She has been a tremendous competitor over the years and on Stroller, in particular, she was unbelievable.

'Ann and Psalm were fantastic and also did a lot for show jumping. Her particular style of riding suited the horse admirably. Another top rider is Caroline Bradley who, as I have said, deserves everything she can get out of the sport. I don't know anyone in show jumping who would deny her anything because she is such a fighter and works so hard. Whenever she has a good round and comes up trumps, even those she has beaten come over and congratulate her and that is how it should be. They don't begrudge that girl anything.

'Another lady who must be remembered is Janou Tissot, who won the Ladies World Championship twice on that phenomenal horse Rocket.

'Debbie Johnsey lives just up the road from me, and the thing that really stands out about her as far as I am concerned is that hers is a great show jumping family and this you have to admire. Her mother and father were always behind her every yard of the way, travelling to shows and helping her whenever they could. She had a couple of good horses in Moxy and Speculator and full marks to her because she could go out and beat the world. You are only as good as your horses and Debbie was always doing well with the ones she had.

'Another young lady who is emerging and one whom I consider has a very bright future is Jane Sergeant. Her parents are behind her, too, and I am sure she will make it. She has a very good style and rides well.

'When I take a long hard look at the ladies in show jumping and am forced to say who I think was the best, I would have to say that I have not seen anyone better than Pat Smythe, who was an artist. She had a lovely way about her and I like to think that I base a lot of my style on Pat. She could win any sort of class and always did it so nicely.

'The ladies used to have their own World Championship, but I didn't much like the event and thought it was a bit of a farce. It went down well at Hickstead, though, and it was probably important to those who rode in it, but I think it is much better as it is now – mixed –

Debbie Johnsey on Classic

for both male and female riders. But I also think that if any of them got through to the final of the World Championship now, they would find the going very tough because it is just that.

'I have also been asked if women project the sport as well as men and, when that happens, I think of my sister Liz. She is as successful as anyone can be but nobody seems to get overexcited in the press about her and she is not built up as a tremendous star by either radio or television. And yet for sheer value she is probably better than any of us.

'There are, of course, a lot of girls who never ride in competition but do a very good job looking after the horses for us. They make good grooms because they are gentle and fall in love with the horses they are looking after. I know all those who have worked for me have always put the horses before any boyfriends.

'And, when we are travelling, they always look after me, making sure I get my bacon sandwiches and regular cups of coffee. Well, if my wife is not on the trip, someone has to look

99

Opposite: *David says that Pat Smythe was the best lady show jumper ever and he bases a lot of his style on hers*

after me, or I would probably starve. Sometimes I am in such a hurry I tend to throw things down when I should be putting them away, and the incredible thing is the less interest I show the more I get looked after.

'As far as food is concerned, I eat too much junk food when Liz is not around to keep an eye on me. My favourite meal, which Liz cooks beautifully, is roast beef and Yorkshire pud – English style.

'Liz doesn't ride the horses in their work because keeping a home and family is enough and a woman can only do so much in a day. It wouldn't be fair to expect her to help with the horses because she has enough to do looking after me and James.

'Liz's best quality, apart from being a wonderful person, is that she understands me and that takes a lot of doing. When I'm going to a show, I just step into the lorry and drive off, packing anything to take with me doesn't enter my head because I'm usually thinking of other things. But Liz always remembers and I cannot recall a time when she has forgotten anything.

'I have to admit that I must be the world's worst husband as far as washing up, decorating the house or gardening is concerned. I put that down to the fact that, when I was ten years old, I took an interest in gardening and growing things but overdid it and ruined my enthusiasm. I would love to do those things but there just isn't time.

'I think Liz will tell you that I did wash up once but now she lets me sit down and watch the television because she considers I work hard enough. Isn't she lovely? Although I don't give James as much time as I would like, I love to play with him and am always giving him piggy-back rides. He's not big enough yet to play football but he will be in time. I wouldn't be without him for the world and yet before I was married I didn't think I could feel like that, but then kids grow on you.

'I have also done things I never thought

James

about before, like the time Liz insisted that I learn to change a nappy and get used to folding the damn thing so it didn't end up around James's ankles. But my fingers went all over the place and I couldn't get hold of it properly. But Liz persisted, her reasoning being that if anything happened to her I should know what to do. I don't think my reply satisfied her: I said I could always take him down to his granny.

'But in the end she did get me doing it properly although I was terrified what I might do with the pin. When I did eventually get it on, she took it off and did it again but was satisfied that at least I had tried. I think she saw it as the Everest of her career getting me to handle that nappy.'

Many men put their wives on pedestals and treat them as someone rather special. Does David treat Liz like this?

'I would love to think I did, but I am sure she would say I don't. The difference is – she is very special to me, and I know it.'

13 Three Times a Champion

There have been many great moments in David's life, and he is a man who takes success firmly in his stride. But there are occasions which mean a lot to him for one reason or another and winning the Benson & Hedges Professional Show Jumping Championships three times, at Cardiff, his home ground, are counted among the best. For it was in this city that he was born, in 1940. The sporting crowds there love him and, whenever he rides before them in the delightful grounds of the castle, where the show takes place, he can be assured of a warm welcome.

'The first one there was in 1974 and it was actually billed as the World Professional Championships. And, in all fairness to those who run it, it was a very good competition because there were a lot of top riders taking part, including America's Rodney Jenkins. It was a new concept in our sport and I was well aware that everyone was taking it very seriously and that became a challenge. The show was held after the Royal International and just before Dublin. I remember my approach to it was one of total dedication and I applied myself to it as much as I did to any other major championship.

'One of the main reasons for this, and one which gave me an added incentive, was the fact that it was held on my home ground. It was also a nice title to pick up if it was at all possible. I worked out my campaign of action and jumped Sportsman for the first two nights and then brought Philco out for the third and final day. In the end, I finished fourth the first evening and third the following night, and, as the results were cumulative, when I was runner-up on Philco in that last leg it gave me the

championship and title, which I must say I was very pleased about.

'It must be said, however, that Rodney Jenkins was very unlucky in the competition and had a fall which knocked him right down the placings, although he did come back and win the Pro-Am Championship at the same show. If it hadn't been for that disaster he might well have won the title I was after, but that's the way it goes for all of us at times.

'The second one I won was in 1978 when I rode Philco on all three days and that really was gratifying because it felt rather special having won it on one horse. But the one that really sticks out in my mind was the one that was staged a year later.

'One of the problems I find with Cardiff is that some of the classes are jumped in the dark and I just happen to have two horses who won't jump in the dark – Queensway's Special and Tabac Original – they get so spooky you wouldn't believe it. They just don't want to know when the light goes.

'It's the same at Windsor. I've gone there and in the dark Tabac Original has done nothing but have faults; and yet, when I bring him out again in daylight to jump in the championship, he comes out and wins. It really is most odd.

'So, in 1979, I had Philco all ready and prepared to the minute for the Cardiff job but at the last moment the poor fella went lame. So I had to use Queensway's Special one night and we had 8 faults, and the next night Tabac Original also had 8 faults. But on the third day the class took place in the afternoon and Tabac walked it and I eventually finished up being sixth. But I am certain it would have been a

totally different story had Philco been available, or those other two competitions had been jumped in daylight. It was, in fact, the worst I had ever done in the championship.

'Last year I rode Philco, who hadn't been at all well but was coming back to form, and before I went to Cardiff I took him to the Three Counties, where he showed that he was approaching his best. But in the actual championship he had a clear round and 3 faults and I finished up being fourth on the first day. Then the heavens opened and the rain bucketed down in torrents. And the fact is Philco doesn't go well in the rain. Then, of all the lovely things to happen, the organizers changed the programme around and brought the evening class forward to about seven o'clock – in daylight – and I was allowed to change my horses and use Tabac Original. He, of course, goes much better in the muck than Philco.

'We had a bit of luck and finished third in that class. The last day's competition was staged in the afternoon as well and when Tabac jumped a clear round most of the opposition had gone. Before the jump-off under the points system there, I couldn't be beaten no matter what I did and it was a lovely feeling.

'Anyway, I went into that jump-off and had a total of 12 faults because the ground was terrible and beginning to hold. Well, he had the first fence down, then the third, and I must admit now that I am the world's worst jockey when I start having fences down. I'm fine when everything is going well, but once they start going wrong I begin to get angry with myself. Luckily on this occasion it was purely academic because we were going to win anyway.

'When I had the third fence down I began to think to myself that it was all useless, but as we came to a set of planks I placed him perfectly. But he went and put in a hell of a twist over the top, landed steep, brought his back up high and went straight into the ground. Well, after that I was going sideways out of the saddle. When he landed, he got stuck in the heavy ground and

by the time he had found his stride again, I was some 2 feet out to the right of him. He saw me there and swerved left and I went straight into the mud. The worst thing was that when I looked back I saw that those wretched planks were still up. The only way to get out of the situation was to laugh my head off and treat it as one huge joke. But I felt a right idiot.

'One of the things I like about Cardiff are the facilities. The stables are excellent and the training areas just right. And, on top of that, it's a nice relaxed programme and everyone goes out of their way to be helpful. There are not too many starters in the classes and I always find the whole thing runs like clockwork.

'But last year one of the spectators had a right go at me and wouldn't stop throwing abuse in my direction. As I went into the arena this old boy kept shouting out, "I know all about you. I remember you from Caldicot," and he never let up, just kept on barracking and I was getting really fed up. It got so bad even the crowd in the stands started booing him, but it never stopped him one little bit.

'In the end I just rode over to him and, as sarcastically as I could, said, "I'm so pleased you could come." But that episode shook me because you just don't expect that sort of thing to happen in our sport. The point was I didn't even know him – had never set eyes on him before.

'Another reason I like Cardiff is that the show is set right in front of the castle, and it does look beautiful. There are also several peacocks about the place which just adds that little extra to the surroundings.

'I don't know, however, what Australian rider Kevin Bacon thinks about the peacocks because one year he was there nothing was going right and, to make matters worse, when one of his horses went to jump a fence, a peacock leapt up from underneath it, and poor Kevin finished up on the floor. But normally they don't get in your way and the horses hardly seem bothered about them.

'I have always loved Cardiff because the fans are right behind you and that is rather special. My whole family attend the show although the

105

*Tabac Original lands David in the mud at the Cardiff
Show 1980 – but they won anyway!*

horses stay there and we go home at night.

'In 1980 the show clashed with Aachen but I hope that has all been sorted out now even though the international calendar is full this year.

'After Cardiff last year, I went to Switzerland to ride, and on that occasion I took Liz with me and we had a lovely time. We even went across to France for lunch and had a couple of pleasant days together. It made a break for both of us. I have been to Switzerland several times and like it enormously.

'One year I went there we jumped on snow which I didn't like too much and the classes started very early – sometimes at eight o'clock – because by lunchtime the snow had begun to melt and it was thought to be dangerous for jumping. So we were getting up at six in the morning to get everything ready and it felt as though it was twenty degrees below.

'It got so bad that Ted Edgar's lorry froze up and it took him several hours to put it right again. After that he decided to run the engine all night so that it wouldn't happen again, and was regularly using about eight gallons of diesel. But it was the only thing he could do under the circumstances.

'When you are show jumping on snow, you have to put studs in the horses' shoes to prevent them from slipping – at the time I am talking about we were fitting bolts. That worked because they were then able to grip but, when I thought about it afterwards, I must admit it made me shudder. Because, if anyone had fallen off and the horse had stepped on his face, it would have been the end because those bolts would probably have torn his head off.

'I do a lot of travelling through the winter and you would be amazed how much a couple of hours flying takes out of you, particularly when you are tired anyway.

'Some of the shows abroad start late and don't finish until the early hours of the morning and after you have had three or four nights of that you feel completely drained. It takes some while before you get your stamina back.

'Although I do a lot of flying during the year I have been lucky enough not to have suffered any bad experiences on a plane. But I know Harvey Smith has. He was going to Berlin once and the aircraft hit an air pocket and his coffee ended up on the roof. One thing I always do though before I get on a plane is ask myself if the journey is really necessary and then I work on the law of averages and convince myself that flying is the safest form of transport. I do, however, like to be in charge of my own destiny whenever possible.

'I remember once going with my sister Liz to Palermo, where we had both been invited to ride, and when we got on the plane I asked her where she would like to sit.

'She replied, "Let's go to the back," and when I inquired why she added, "Because you never hear of an aeroplane reversing into a mountain!" There wasn't an answer to that.'

14 Father Fred

David's father Fred is one of those equestrian experts you meet once, or maybe twice, in a lifetime. He is a member of a rare breed of people who have grown up with horses and he has forgotten more than most will ever know about them. His children follow faithfully in his footsteps. He has, also, the ability to pass on his knowledge and, under his enthusiastic and painstaking guidance, David has become one of the best showjumping riders this nation has ever known. The formative years in David's life are well worth recording and they show that the young man who was much later to become such a brilliant rider didn't always have things easy. His father Fred tells of the good times, the hard days and the moments of absolute delight.

'Right from the beginning when I used to ride in show jumping events and point-to-pointing the English boys would always stick it across us and say we could only jump bean sticks in Wales. And, perhaps they were right because they came along and licked us time and time again. Well, I made up my mind that when I got married and had children I would

Fred Broome at home with David and
Queensway's Big Q

teach them to ride at a very early age so that it would be as natural as walking to them. This I did with David at the tender age of two on Shetland ponies. Within one year he had advanced to Welsh section As, which were bought from a man named Griffiths. I used to strap David on so that he wouldn't fall off and within a few months I was able to take the back straps off – then the side ones came off and he was free to ride on his own.

'In those early days he came on very, very quickly and we went to lots of show classes where he did well. But I may have thought he was a bit too good then because I was breaking ponies and putting him on and then one day things went wrong for him. I had a blood pony which kept on bucking him off and, after this happened a few times, as he has told you, he came to me and said that he wasn't going to ride any more. That shook me a little but I told him that I understood and that it was all right and not to worry. Then I sold the ponies.

'After that I carried on show jumping, and much later at a show near Cardiff David was there and I won the class. When I returned to the box and put the horse away he came up to me and said, "Dad, I think I would like another pony."

'I was delighted that the bad times had passed for him and just replied, "Good – I'll get you one next week."

'He didn't know that I had waited a long time to hear him say that; but I always knew that I mustn't push him into renewing his interest. It had to come from him, in his own time, and when it happened I was delighted. I wanted him to make the first move without any outside help. After he had, I went out and bought him a pony for £14, and within forty-eight hours he was riding it and two weeks later was hunting with me and jumping fences I didn't want him to jump. At first I thought he was rushing things but, from that moment on, you just couldn't stop him in the hunting field.

'Then I started polishing him, showing him how to ride into a fence and so forth. In those days I would work the ponies because I had a lot of patience and would also school them. But

I never jumped them. David would do that two or three days before a show and when he went into the ring I would just amble up to him and say, "Mind you bloody well win." This was something I learnt from Colonel Sir Michael Ansell, when I used to go away with the teams. He would always send that same message by telegram and on many occasions we complied with his wishes and did just what he asked.

'All through my life I have had a very strong will to win and it is this that I have tried hard to pass on to my children. We couldn't afford to lose in those early days and that is why I, too, rode in open gymkhanas when David was competing, because we had to get our entry money back. And that is exactly what we did many times – because we would both play like hell, and win. On the way home we always used to add everything up and work out how much we had spent on petrol or diesel and see if we had made a profit or not. This was one of the ways I hoped to build David's character and that strong will to win. Looking back, I firmly believe this helped to create his ability and his desire to succeed in competitions.

'One of his greatest assets is his ability to relax and he can go in last in a team when he has to have a clear to win and nothing, but nothing, worries him. He goes and does exactly what is required without getting into a panic and that is of the utmost importance. I think this all came about because he was taught properly at a very early age, and even now I tell all sportsmen – whether they are in golf, cricket, boxing or athletics – to teach their children properly because, if they do, their offspring will nearly always be better than they are. It is just a question of teaching – that is so important to me because it helps to shape their characters and put them on the right road to success.

'I always had great ambitions for David and my other children, Elizabeth, Mary and Fred, and it was always a dream of mine to make up an Olympic team with them and win a gold medal, but I didn't quite get there. However, it has given both my wife and myself a lot of pleasure watching them grow up and doing so well. As far as I am concerned, they have made an old man happy and I am very proud of them.

'David was always very good as a boy but, of course, as he got older and started riding big horses he started going to two- and three-day shows. Well, at those meetings the lads tend to wander off a bit; the one-day shows were all right because there were no parties and we would all get on fine. But then we would get some of the longer shows, someone would throw a party and I would have a job to get them back in time. It was difficult to make them think, when they were having a good time, that the following day was when we had to be on top. They had to sacrifice something and on occasions did miss out on a good time at night. They had to be back by 11.30 so they could be fresh the next day and put into practice all those hard, early years of training. It *was* hard for them, but they knew it was right.

'My father was a good horseman and I learnt a lot from him and others and by travelling as much as I could. Then, that knowledge I gained was passed on to David. Because he learnt at a very early age, riding did, eventually, become natural to him – just like walking. His style is good but it is something everyone can achieve if they concentrate hard and work at it like he does. You only get out of life what you put in, because there are never any short cuts where sport is concerned. If you don't have the application, the only person you cheat is yourself.

'It is my firm belief that it is all up to parents to have the discipline and teach youngsters everything that is right. That, in fact, is the making of it all.

'The most satisfying competition I have seen David ride in was the 1960 Olympics in Rome when we were lucky enough to have that great horse Sunsalve. We were given a fortnight to produce him, which we did at White City by finishing second and then winning two competitions, including the King George V Gold Cup, and that was a great success. Then David went to Rome with Sunsalve, won a bronze medal and gave me one of the greatest pleasures of my life. The other wonderful moment came in 1970 at La Baule, in France, during the World Championships, when David rode Douglas Bunn's Beethoven. He was a very good horse with a bit of the devil in him, but that didn't worry us too much because that is just how we like them. I used to ride him in for David and school him and, at those World Championships, I did exactly that before he went into the ring.

'Well, he won the world title because nobody else could quite ride the horse like David – nothing like, in fact, although they tried hard enough. I will never forget that day because after he had won I just walked away, went and sat on the collecting ring rail and cried. The tears just streamed down my face, I forgot everything and then went and missed the presentation ceremony!

'One of the things I find great about David is that he is always prepared to listen to anything I have to say to him. Once I have given him some advice I will often see him putting it into practice afterwards and that gives me a lot of satisfaction. I sometimes get the impression that he thinks, "Well, the old man might be right."

'I can often see myself in him, because as a young man I had the same ambitions and enthusiasm as he has. One of the greatest moments in my life was beating Harry Llewellyn and Foxhunter not once, but twice, and that felt very good.

'I have always told David that, to keep a horse going and good enough to win, he must always have it balanced and moving in rhythm, on a shortish stride. If you have got that you can jump anything, even off a short stride. The whole basis of being successful is making sure you have that combination and, if a horse has those qualities, he can go anywhere and do anything. It is as simple as that. I never really taught David anything about speed – only that he had always to be aware in classes that required speed that he had to cut corners and come off the bends with his horse on the right leg, so that he met the next fence properly. But everyone can make mistakes in such classes –

even Harvey Smith – and, when that happens, the competition is lost.

'But David has always had what I can only describe as a clock in his head and, although he often gives the public the impression that he is going slowly, or slower than anyone else, it is not the case because more often than not he ends up winning. It really is incredible on occasions. I still like to think, however, that most of the success is due to the fact that he is turning the horse properly, keeping it on the

right leg and placing him at his fences correctly. He keeps the horse well together so it is literally bouncing and full of impulsion. One reason for this is that he knows that, if he dies on the horse, or messes things up, the horse has no hope of winning.

'I may have helped David a lot, but my wife has also played her part in his success because she balanced things up very well. I would always be taking the children to shows but she kept an eye on me and told me, "You can't have them all the time. They must do their schooling and their exams." And, on many occasions, she wouldn't let me have them at all and that was a good thing when you think

Fred Broome with Bess and her foal. Both David and Liz Edgar had a lot of success on Bess in the sixties when they were first starting out in show jumping

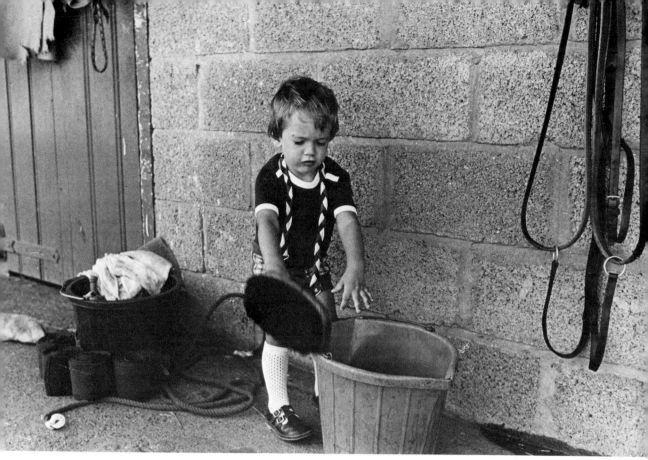

about it. If anything had happened to them and they were not successful with horses, or had been injured, at least they would have had their education to fall back on. That is why my wife was so very right to make sure their schooling never suffered at all.

'When David did go show jumping with me I always made sure, as he has mentioned, that he watched Pat Smythe, because she did have that rhythm and balance that I have been talking about. She could come round on short strides, keeping the horses just right and I always considered that she was a great lady to watch show jumping. I know David learnt an awful lot from her – not by asking, but just by watching her compete. In my opinion, in the early sixties, there were really only two people who could ride against the clock, and, when someone once asked Pat Smythe who the other one was, she was said to have replied, "That little Welsh boy."

'Looking back over the years, I must

Fred would be delighted to help James follow in his father's footsteps and has already bought him a pony called Pip

mention that another memorable moment for the whole family came when David was awarded the OBE. It gave me a lot of satisfaction because I had always thought that being presented with such an award was an impossibility for the Broome family and, when we were told that it was actually to happen, it was a wonderful feeling.'

Everyone in show jumping knows only too well that Fred Broome has helped David enormously during his career, and the big question all who are interested in the sport want to know is would he do the same for his grandson James if he, like his father, had the desire to ride show jumping? It would mean that the family history would be repeating what happened with Fred and his father and David.

'I'm sure I would like to help James, there is

no question about that, and I have already bought him a pony called Pip. He is a section A pony and it was rather interesting how I came to find him. I went to Cardigan looking for some black Welsh cobs to make up my team and a man said he had one down in Fishguard which sounded just what I wanted. But when I got there it wasn't what I needed. But running with it was this lovely little pony who did impress me. Well, when I asked the man about him, I was told that the pony's pedigree was full of champions but that he was owned by his wife and daughter; if I was interested, I would have to go back to the house and discuss the matter with them. I had a meal with the family, but getting the man to say how much he wanted for the pony was awful because he wanted me to bid for him. I always like people to tell me how much they want, then we can start negotiating. Eventually I bought the pony for £85 and he is a little gem with a great character, and James is getting on well with him. I'm sure that both David and myself will help James all we can – David, in particular, because no matter how good you are there always comes a day when someone turns up who is better. But, if you have trained your own child to take your place, it is wonderful – that I know from experience.

'I think that David has helped show jumping because people get a lot of pleasure watching him ride. We have, by being in the sport, also learnt a lot from it and know how to treat horses properly and as they should be treated. Look after them in show jumping and they will look after you because they fall in love with it and go well for you. If they make a mistake, it is no use at all getting angry because everyone at some time or another makes mistakes. When things do go wrong the only thing to do is keep on persevering with them until they get it right.

'I think one of the main reasons David has been so successful *is* because he treats his horses with respect and has been taught that, even if he loses a competition, the thing to do is come out of the ring smiling and take it like a good sportsman. Never, never blame the horse. That helps build character and we both hope that he has been a good ambassador for the sport.

'He has never, ever, given a horse a good hiding in or out of the ring, and the secret which has stood him in good stead all these years is schooling his horses properly. They are like children in many ways; they have to respect you, and you must be firm but fair with them – then they will grow to love the sport and do their best for you. It is nice to know that horses do behave well, even though they may come out and give a buck or two or have a bit of a lark; but they settle down and, if they have been looked after properly, they will give the best of their ability. David has found that out and that is one of the reasons he has done so very well.'

15 Tributes from Around the World

One of the best ways to find out the true worth of a man is to ask those who know him, or something about him, for their opinions. Apart from talking to the people David meets practically every day, I went to West Germany and, at the Aachen International show, spoke to riders from many parts of the world. I met them individually and no one knew what the others had said. The results, I think, are incredible and are proof, if any were needed, that David is a man held in high regard by all those who have ever met him. The two main questions were, 'What do you think of David Broome as a rider?' and 'What do you think of him as a man?' The replies are remarkable because they nearly all adopt the same theme and show that he could go practically anywhere in the world where show jumping takes place and meet a friend. That is the measure of his popularity.

Dennis Murphy (America)

'I think David dominates the sport and is a winner all the way. Everyone would like to be like him. You have to admire the man because he is fantastic and if you are ever lucky enough to beat him it makes you feel good.'

François Mathy (Belgium)

'I first met him in Aachen when he was riding Sunsalve and I think he won all there was to win at the show. I was very impressed with him and I think he sets a good example to young riders. He is sympathetic to his horses and keeps them a long time. David is a good man and will never sell anyone a bad horse. If it isn't right, he will tell them so and that is another

reason why the people he knows remain friends with him for many years. He and his family are all honest people and that makes life so much easier for everyone else. As a rider, I think he is the best.'

Ronnie Massarella (British chef d'équipe)

'The man is brilliant and I don't think there will be another like him. When I left him out of that Nations Cup team at Hickstead, I was almost physically sick. Not many people realized that but, if I had picked the wrong team, there were those who would have jumped on me. I remember five or six years ago at Wembley I did the same thing to him, but on that occasion exclusion from the team meant that he couldn't qualify for one of the other major classes there. Well, I had made my decision and that was that, although David did come back to me and asked if I would reconsider. I hadn't realized at the time that leaving him out meant he couldn't ride in the event he really wanted to and, when he asked me again, I walked away, told him I would think about it, but knew that there was no way I could change my mind. When I went back and told him, he smiled and said, "If you had done so you would have gone right down in my estimation."

'Now you can understand why I like him so much. Another of his great qualities is being able to cope with pressure. When he is on British teams, he puts other riders before himself. A classic example of what I am talking about came in the 1978 World Championships at Aachen, in West Germany. It was then that he approached me and explained that he wouldn't be concentrating too hard on the

Ronnie Massarella, the British chef d'équipe, with the successful 1979 European Championships team

individual title because he thought it right that the team should win, if it could, because then everyone would share in the success. I will never forget that gesture as long as I live.'

John Whitaker (Britain)

'David's been at the top for a long time and has done a lot for show jumping. Apart from that, he has also helped me a lot and not only with riding, but personally as well. He always wants to put other people before himself.'

Billy Ringrose (former International rider and Ireland's chef d'équipe)

'He has a great personality and thinks deeply about what he is doing, even though he always appears to be casual and cool about things. I think that is one of the reasons for his longevity in the sport, plus the fact that over the years he has been able to adapt to changes and is always ready to accept advice. Out of the ring he is happy and has the ability to relax. He's a nice fella all round.'

Tim Grubb (Britain)

'As far as I am concerned he is Mr Nice Guy and I don't think that anyone could have anything bad to say about him. Sure he likes money, but then he is a professional and entitled to win what he can. Even if you beat him, as long as you do it fairly, he is the first to come over and congratulate you. Some people might even say that he goes abroad a lot and that they should be given their chance, but he beats the backsides off all of them because he is the best in the world and so should keep going abroad on British teams.'

Sonke Sonksen (West Germany)

'I have know David a long time and he is a very fair man and well liked in Germany.'

Nelson Pessoa (Brazil)

'He is a good winner and a good loser and I try to be the same. He is a great horseman who treats his horses right. I have to follow his career from a distance, but I much admire the man because he uses science when he rides.'

Frederic Cottier (France)

'I know he is the best and a man who is kind and open. We like him in France, not just because he has good results but because he is a good person. Two years ago in Germany he helped me with one of my horses when I was riding it in a hackamore and having problems. He told me what I should do and I was able to correct the fault. He likes to help others.'

Toshimi Hirasawa (Japan)

'David Broome is very good. We read all about him in books and look at pictures of his horses.'

Jesus Gomez Portugal (Mexico)

'I met David when he was riding in the 1968 Mexico Olympics and took him to different places to show him my country. At one of these places of interest we stayed at a beautiful hacienda which had one hundred rooms and we shared one. Also there were American and Canadian teams. In the evenings I used to tease David and make jokes with him and I can say that he is great fun. We would fight with pillows and I can tell you that he is the best pillow thrower in the world.

'He will always be welcome to Mexico because the people like him. Some riders they find very hard to get along with, but he is nice and easy and a very good friend. As a rider, he is good and has a lot of stamina for winning. He also has style and natural ability and gives me the impression he completely understands every one of his horses. The one thing that I remember is how he rode Fidux in the 1970 World Championships in La Baule. He had to ride three other horses as well in the competition but Fidux was the hardest. David made him relax even though the horse was very strong. He has good hands and makes it all look so easy.'

Luis Alvarez Cervera (Spain)

'Everything I could possibly say about him would be too little. To start with he is first and foremost a horseman who cares about his horses and is always worrying about the ground and wondering if it will be too hard or too soft for them. When he is riding he takes his time to get them how he wants them and he has a deep knowledge of his horses and the competitions in which he rides. I admire the way he always keeps them on the bridle and bouncing and never asks them to do too much. When he wins he does so by fractions of a second, so that it does not take too much out of them. When I first started show jumping he would always speak to me and ask how things were with my horses. Although he is a famous man he does not have a star complex. He's a champion in all ways and a good friend to every rider.'

Thomas Fuchs (Switzerland)

'There may be others who are very successful but they never keep their horses for so long. He seems to maintain the same rhythm and just does enough when he is jumping for them to clear a fence by only a small margin, rather than by feet. That way he keeps them longer and doesn't wear them out. It is not possible to say anything bad about him.'

Janusz Bobik (Poland)

'He is different from other riders and has a very good eye for horses. If they are making mistakes he can put everything right in five minutes. I first met him in Aachen a few years back and two years ago worked for him for four months. There is something special between him and his horses and I know he is a friendly person.'

Marian Kozicki (Poland)

'He is a super rider – among the five best in the world.'

Paul Schockemohle (West Germany)

'David wins too much. But he is my best friend in show jumping and I cannot say anything bad about him. He has won everything in the world and is still the same person – very straight and

Alwin Schockemohle and Johan Heins chat during the 1979 European Championships in Rotterdam

honest. A lot of people think he is just a rider but he is more than that; he is also a personality, but at the same time a very private man. As president of the International Riders Club he has done a lot of good because he uses his brains and does everything perfectly. When I am arguing, I usually follow my instincts, but he is very serious and that is why he is right for president. When we have committee meetings, he will talk for hours to people and can change their minds without their losing face. He treats people right but I know he can be very strong.'

Johan Heins (Holland – A former Individual European Champion)

'David has the best reputation in show jumping; he is always consistent in his behaviour and an unbelievable horseman. He also has courage because, if he thinks the courses are too big for his horses, he will withdraw them because he puts them before anything else. I know he has helped me a lot and even now I ask his advice – which he always gives. David never has problems with other people and for me is the greatest.'

Alwin Schockemohle (West Germany)

'For me he is the best in the world and has been so for a long time. I first met him when he was riding horses like Wildfire and Sunsalve. He is the best horseman: a man who is always very fair to his horses and who is a fantastic manager of them, giving them a rest when they need it and giving them time to become what they can. He is a horseman *par excellence*. We have had many battles and David has always been a good winner and a good loser because he is fair. We are good friends and I know that if I was in trouble he would help me. I think he is like a brother. If we had more people like him in the world there would never be any problems. The whole family – mother, Papa Broome and sisters Mary and Liz and his brother Fred – is how a family should be. They all work together and are good to other people. When David retires I think he would make a good chef d'équipe, because he knows everything there is to know about horses.'

Hans Gunter Winkler (West Germany)

'I have know him since 1955 and for me he is a wonderful sportsman and the most consistent competitor on the international show jumping scene. He has ridden in the Olympics and all kinds of championships, has won medals and is one of the great people at shows. Besides this, he shows his quality on different horses from the time of Sunsalve to Philco, and on the right horse is one of the hardest men to beat. He is a great person and for sure among the best four riders in the world since the Second World War.'

16 What the Future Holds

Unlike footballers or cricket players, show jumping riders do not have huge savings waiting for them when they retire, and as a consequence they must look after their own interests when the time comes for them to stop competing. The majority will not have big, fat cheques to put in the bank and for many the going will be tough. That is why David has thought long and hard about the question of settling down and doing something else.

'I intend to keep in business with my brother and by the time I come to retire from riding I hope it will be lucrative. It's hard work at the moment, but one does have to think about the future and over the next few years I hope to build the farm up to such an extent that it will help keep me and my family. I don't think it will ever be as financially rewarding as show jumping has been but I intend to see that everything will be all right for them.

'The funny thing is everyone keeps asking me when I intend to give up, but the plain truth is I cannot afford to do so at the present time. I know it will have to come eventually, and I would like to see myself in a little bit of business, but with the farm as my bread and butter. When it is time for me to go, I know I will not have a show which invites people to "Come and watch David Broome's last round in show jumping" because I can see myself simply disappearing from the scene slowly. You have just got to be sensible about everything and if you find that you cannot win at the big shows then the obvious thing to do is not go to them. But, having been in the sport a long time, I would find it a terrible wrench just to stop one day and forget all about show jumping. I just don't think that could happen.

'After all, show jumping is a part of me and I think will always be, and what I intend to do

when the time is right is get a novice and go to a show on a Saturday afternoon with my wife and son James, who perhaps will ride in the junior classes. We would do the cycle all over again – just like my father did – a sort of continuation of the family history. That would please my father, I know, and it is something that I would very much like to happen. After all, I don't see why one should have all these big, dramatic giving-up sessions.

'Just think for a moment of the Horse of the Year show at Wembley. How could I ever not go to one of those? If it was ever announced there that it was to be my last one, it just wouldn't be right unless I happened to die the very next day. It's okay, I suppose, if you happen to be a little bit sentimental, but I am afraid that is just not my scene at all. I don't like tear-jerkers and, for me, saying goodbye to everything I have known for so long would be the hard part.

'I look at it this way; if you are not good at something, you don't do it anyway, but why not carry on as long as you can? When I eventually stop, as we all must at some stage of our lives, I will miss a few places but certainly not the hustle and bustle because, when you get a bit older, you find that you don't want to be dashing about all over the place like you did when you were younger.

'But I am sure that, when I give up, there will be so much for me to do on the farm and in business to fill my life that I can get on with it and not think I am wasting my time at the show jumping lark.'

At the moment David is doing very well and riding better than ever. But does it sometimes worry him that he might lose that edge and start to go downhill?

'Yes, of course. That is just a matter of time

because nobody can stay as good as they once were and nobody can retain the drive to keep them going for ever. It's just a matter of common sense and facing up to reality and if you do that then life must get that much easier. Youngsters have more drive because they havn't worn themselves out doing it all before and are always fresh and keen. For example, last year was my twentieth Bath and West Show; now that's not like someone going there to ride for the second time. Certainly I have had more experience, but youngsters are hungry for success and will probably do well because of that.'

Does David feel that he would like to help young people by coaching them?

'That is a very good idea and one which is very close to my heart. But good riders do not always make good trainers or coaches, though it would be a useful source of income. There was a very funny instance when a friend rang me once to say that someone he knew was having trouble with her horse and could I possibly help her out and correct the faults. Well, they duly turned up – the young girl and her horse – and I started to tell her what she should be doing so that they would jump a combination properly. The problem was they were going too fast into them, so I fixed up a few grids and told her to get the horse steadied up a bit and showed her how to work the animal. After a few sessions like that, I told her to go away for a week, then come back and show me how she was getting on, riding the way I had told her. Well, away she went and I didn't think any more about it until several days later when my wife told me the girl's mother had been on the phone and said that the youngster wouldn't be coming back to me again because, since she had had the lesson, the horse hadn't completed a round at show jumping; it kept on being eliminated and, on reflection, she didn't think it was worthwhile taking any more instruction. You can't win them all, but I had to have a little snigger about that one because the lady was obviously sincere and I was getting the blame for her daughter's horse stopping. That really put me in my place and was so much for the "great teacher Broome". From that experience and others, it really does go to show that good riders don't always make good teachers – not because they don't know what they are talking about.

'The main thing to remember is that everyone has their own way of doing things, which cannot easily be explained to anyone else. You might be a brilliant competitor yourself but what suits you might be completely wrong for someone else and, if that is the case, it doesn't really matter how much you school a pupil – they will never be any better. When Jack Talbot Ponsonby was around he used to advise riders to do this, that and the other, and I always thought you should listen carefully to what he and others had to say and then mix it with your own thoughts. That way you can get the best of both worlds and with any luck learn something that will be of benefit to you. In my experience, what people tend to do is follow a teacher's instructions to the letter without thinking at all for themselves and, when they actually fall short of what should be done, they cock it up and then blame him for being a complete idiot.

'What they don't seem to realize is that you cannot teach anyone to be a good rider, or school a horse properly, in five minutes. It takes a great deal of time and patience and, if they haven't got that to start with, what hope is there of ever putting them on the right track? When someone is having a moan, it generally means that they haven't listened properly to what has been said and then they need someone to blame. It's human nature. But the fall guy every time is the poor trainer whose only aim in life is to make things right and easier for those under his charge. I am a firm believer in listening properly to anyone – even a fool – providing you add to what has been said with something you know is right and has worked in the past for you.

'With enough care and understanding it is nearly always possible to put right the bad faults the rider, or their horse, may have, but what you cannot do is force people to listen and digest the information you are giving them.

That can only be done by them and, if they don't really want to learn, what hope have they got? But, yes, I would have a crack at teaching because it would be a good way of helping others and would be a source of income for me.

'At the moment, though, I am happy to keep on riding and, hopefully, winning and, when the time comes for me to stop, I will understand because I know I can't go on for ever.'

We all know that riders, like great athletes, one day have to bow to the master of time, but what they have given us during their careers can never be forgotten because it will always be in our hearts or printed very clearly in the record books.

David Broome has been a master of show jumping, a perfect example of how we should all try to be as members of the human race and a credit to the sport he loves. For me, he is one of the greatest riders of our time and a man who will always be remembered because he was fair, honest and, above all, put his horses before anything else.

Index